THE ART OF FRIENDSHIP

Roger Horchow

Sally Horchow

The ART of
FRIENDSHIP

The ART of
FRIENDSHIP

70 Simple Rules for Making Meaningful Connections

ROGER HORCHOW
SALLY HORCHOW

foreword by
MALCOLM GLADWELL

Neiman Marcus

Exclusive Neiman Marcus Edition

To all the people in our lives with whom we've made meaningful connections: we are so fortunate to call you our friends.

A Quirk Packaging Book
119 West 23rd Street, Suite 1001
New York, NY 10011
www.quirkpackaging.com

Designed by Lynne Yeamans and Nancy Leonard
Edited by Signe Bergstrom

Manufactured in the U.S.A.

10 9 8 7 6 5 4 3 2 1

ISBN 0-9770219-0-4

CONTENTS

FOREWORD

I first met Sally Horchow at a dinner party in New York an embarrassingly long time ago. Sally was far and away the most interesting person in the room, and I will confess that I had an immediate crush on her. She did not, as it turned out, have a crush on me—or maybe she was distracted by some pre-existing crush. I don't know. As I recall, there was a day when I was traveling and trying to call her at her office from the airport in an attempt to set up a date—in that desperate, headlong way that young men tend to do-and it slowly began to dawn on me that *it was not happening.* Oh well, I thought, in my disappointment, that's that. But here's the thing: that wasn't that. I was in.

We have a tendency, I think, to pretend that the social arts are a good deal more complicated and mysterious than they actually are. When someone is charismatic, we say that they have that indefinable *something.* When someone is beautiful and charming, we skip to the French—that *jais ne sais quois.* Whatever it is that happens when we meet someone-and when some kind of conclusion is drawn by one party about another—is treated as a big black box. "I don't know what happened," the hapless guy always says, when he returns home from the unexpectedly fun first date, "but we had a lot of fun."

But the truth is that the thing that happens between two

people is not a black box. Friendship, like crime, is a simple matter of means, motive, and opportunity. You must have a certain amount of social technique. You must have the desire to be open to another. And you must be in a position to meet someone new. Talk to a seasoned detective about the crimes that he has seen in his lifetime, and chances are that he will tell you—in sharp contrast to what we learn on the television cop shows—that there are few surprises in a crime scene. Well, there is nothing surprising about friendship either. Sally and I moved effortlessly to the level of friendship because Sally accepted me as her friend. We liked each other enough to want to have each other around in our lives, in whatever shape or form that would take—and Sally was graceful and generous and gifted enough in the social arts to make that happen. It was as simple as that.

I wrote a big chunk of my first book on Sally's couch, house-sitting for her while she took off on one of her periodic jaunts around the globe. That's one definition of friendship: generosity. I met Sally's father, Roger, through her, and put him in an article I was writing for the *New Yorker* (on, appropriately enough, people who are really good at making friends). We sat in his apartment in New York and chatted happily for a few hours, and I left knowing that I was now in with him as well. Like daughter, like father. At the end of the long and exhausting promotional tour for my second book, I found myself in Austin, Texas, lonely and awkward at a party where I thought I knew no one. Then, to my delight, across the room I spotted Sally's friends Eve and Keven. Because they were Sally's friends, I knew—right away—that they could be my friends, too. After all, I was in.

The book that follows is an exercise in the demystification of friendship. It is a guide to the rules of the game—and "game" is an inappropriate word, because the premise of what Sally and her father have written is that the art of friendship has a few simple guidelines that anyone can be taught, the way that anyone can be taught how to play gin rummy or to dance the samba. Of course—particularly in the latter case—it's a good deal easier to learn something that looks very difficult from the outside if you're being taught by an expert. But trust me, in the case of the Horchows senior and junior, you're in the hands of experts.

—*Malcolm Gladwell*

Only connect.

—E.M. FORSTER

Forster had it right: no friendship was ever hatched without making a real connection with another person. Finding common ground, a similar sense of humor or taste, or a mutual interest—these are the things that bring us together. But before the joys of friendship can ensue, we must meet our friends. And before we meet them, we must find them. What is the internal sense that points out potential friends in our midst? Is it something we're born with, or is it an instinct possessed by only truly outgoing people?

When Roger started the mail-order catalog, *The Horchow Collection*, little did he know that his greatest legacy and accomplishment in life would be, instead, the "Horchow Connection"—something our friend Malcolm Gladwell explores in his book *The Tipping Point*. Roger, Malcolm writes, is a "connector," one of those rare "people with a special gift for bringing the world together," a person "with a truly extraordinary knack of making friends and acquaintances." Although he also said connectors were "people who know a lot of people," he pointed out that Roger was someone who cultivated acquaintances and friendships simply for the joy of doing so.

The description was flattering, and, if we do say so, true, except for one thing: we believe that anyone can be a "connector." It may be an instinctive skill for some, but it's one that can certainly be acquired by others. If you can learn to be a person who takes action in any of the ways we describe, if you make the nurturing of friendships a personal priority, and if you understand the importance of following up with people, you will enjoy vital and long-lasting relationships in your life.

This book contains seventy basic rules for making and maintaining connections. These principles of friendship have been distilled from a long lifetime of experience on Roger's part, and have been further tested and refined by Sally, as a connector of the next generation. In writing this book together and putting the rules into print, we hope to offer would-be connectors of every generation a set of practical tools for building meaningful relationships in the modern world.

Since taking action and following up is the essence of making and keeping friends, for each rule, we provide an action point that will help you put the rule into practice. We urge you to try them out—or develop your own, geared to your particular situation.

In addition, sidebars (red for Roger, pink for Sally) describe specific experiences we have had that either led us to develop a particular rule or illustrate how they work in real life situations. We claim no special education in the subject beyond what life has taught us; we are neither sociologists nor scientists. Nevertheless, the rules we outline have been used successfully by at least two generations of users—and here are the stories to prove it!

The early chapters of the book focus on how to make new friends, from searching out those special someones with whom you have an affinity to building the foundations of a lasting relationship. In the middle chapters, we discuss the care and maintenance of friendships—including how to keep longstanding relationships fresh. Finally, we delve into advanced friendship, which includes handling more complicated relationships and knowing when to quit.

We haven't made too much distinction between personal friendships and business relationships; for the most part, these rules apply to both. We have found that the basic underpinnings of a strong relationship—mutual respect, shared interests, and joint activities—are as applicable to business alliances as they are to personal friendships.

We also believe that a meaningful connection does not necessarily have to always imply a lifelong, devoted friendship—there is room in every life for fulfilling acquaintanceships, situational friendships, and temporary but mutually beneficial associations. Understanding these different levels of friendship is an important part of making healthy connections.

Interestingly, one of the pleasures of undertaking this father-daughter project was that we found our own connection deepening as we learned new things about each other over the course of writing the manuscript. We hope that reading this book will help you to become a successful connector, too.

—*Roger Horchow and Sally Horchow*

CHAPTER ONE

Make the Connection

Sir, I look upon every day to be lost
in which I do not make a new acquaintance.
—SAMUEL JOHNSON

Think about it: with 365 days in the year and countless people in the world, there are myriad opportunities for you to meet a potential friend, so long as you are looking for him or her. Who knows? At this very moment, your soon-to-be best friend may be sitting across from you. But you'll never know it unless you're open to the encounter. So look up. Say hello. Remember, some of the best friendships are borne of unusual circumstances or in curious settings. So, keep your guard down and your friendship antennae up—you never know where and when a potential friend may be found.

REACH OUT TO SOMEONE YOU DON'T KNOW

No friendship was ever launched without making that first connection. You've got to find some kind of common ground— a passion for surfing, say, or for Bill Murray movies (especially the flops), or even kiddie breakfast cereals. Of course, before you discover that shared love of Frosted Flakes, you've got to meet your new potential friends, and before that, you've got to find them.

So where *can* you unearth these like-minded individuals? A better question is, where can't you find them? The secret lies in truly being open to making the connection. If you are willing to strike up a conversation, you could meet someone in line at the post office, ordering a Decaf Java Chip Frappuccino at Starbucks, or scoping the decorations at an office Christmas party. Almost any spot has friend-making potential. The first step in making friends is simply to place yourself amongst people you don't know, or don't know well (something most of us do every day, without even being aware of it) and then start talking. Good intentions and halfhearted efforts don't make connections; a genuine commitment to treating every situation as an opportunity to meet someone new does.

☐ *Speak to someone you've never met.*

HONE YOUR "FRIENDSHIP ANTENNAE"

But, you may be thinking, I'm in places where I'm surrounded by strangers everyday—where are all these new friends you're promising me? Rest assured, the friends are there. It's all a matter of having your "friendship antennae" up and at the ready. Now, we don't mean the coil-spring, bobble-topped headbands you find at the costume shop (those, sadly, may cost you new friends, or at least earn you ones you'd rather not have.) No, we mean an invisible set of antennae that all of us—not just your annoyingly outgoing colleagues—are born with. These antennae represent your instinct for friendship, and they should be on the alert right now, even as you read this.

Of course, the problem is that in most potential meeting places—whether the office lunchroom, the bookstore's "mystery" aisle, or the annual New Year's party—you aren't always ready to connect with strangers. And yet these ordinary moments are precisely when your antennae should be up. Here's how to do it: look around at the people nearby. Does anyone seem interesting to you? Perhaps someone is reading the latest Patricia Cornwell—the very one you just finished. Or you've spotted a person with a great bicycle that you'd love to know more about. Those are potential friends—and you've begun to hone your friendship antennae.

☐ *Look for extraordinary friends in ordinary places.*

IT TAKES ALL KINDS

Friendship is not always easily defined. There is a range of meaningful relationships, and not all of them need to be of the close, call-you-up-in-the-middle-of-the-night variety to be worthwhile. For example, you might have been taking the same yoga class for several years, and frequently afterward you and a fellow yogi go for a frozen yogurt and chat about the class. You've never been to each other's homes or met each other's family but you enjoy your weekly fifteen minutes together and would feel disappointed if you didn't do it. Is your yoga buddy a friend? Of course. Do you need to deepen the relationship? Not unless you both want to.

There are plenty of other types of friendships that are meaningful but not necessarily profound or long-term. Work friendships, situational friendships, cordial acquaintance-ships—the varieties are as plentiful as the people you meet. Each type of friend should be treated with respect and the appropriate level of affection. If you stay open to the possibilities for friendships that do not necessarily conform to the most common expectations, you are likely to engage in some rewarding interactions that you would otherwise miss out on.

☐ *Redefine your concept of friendship and see*
if you can add a few people to your list of friends.

LOOK FOR CLUES

If some of the suggestions in this book sound like an anxious mother advising her single daughter to always be on the lookout for the man of her dreams, that's because they arise from the same instinct: that urge to connect. In the case of seeking out friends, the connection is platonic, though a deep friendship may be as emotionally fulfilling as a romantic relationship.

Finding the "friend of your dreams" can be as simple as keeping your eyes wide open. "Some Enchanted Evening," a song from *South Pacific* that's all about recognizing these moments, said it all:

Some enchanted evening, you may see a stranger
You may see a stranger across a crowded room
And somehow you know, you know even then
That somewhere you'll see her again and again
Some enchanted evening, someone may be laughing
You may hear her laughing across a crowded room
And night after night, as strange as it seems
The sound of her laughter will sing in your dreams
Who can explain it, who can tell you why
Fools give you reasons, wise men never try
Some enchanted evening, when you find your true love
When you feel her call you across a crowded room

Then fly to her side and make her your own
Or all through your life you may dream all alone
Once you have found her, never let her go
Once you have found her, never let her go

Of course, in meeting a friend (and in life outside a musical), there is perhaps a little less urgency. But the sentiment—to act on those inexplicable connections to people—still holds true. With your antennae at high frequency, you can pick up on clues that will point you toward your potential friend.

In short, learn to trust—and act on—your first impressions. If you happen to show up at a dinner party wearing the same dress (or necktie) as someone else, don't take it as a cause for embarrassment. You've just found a potential friend with similar, and possibly impeccable, taste. Similarly, should you see someone reading a book you loved, consider asking him how he likes it. Or if you see the same person every day during your morning jog, say hello. You never know where the conversation might lead.

☐ *Pick out the most promising potential friend in*
a room and observe him or her. If you seem to have
something in common, start a conversation.

RULE **#5**

Use a "Pick-Up Line"

Making the next move is the most important step in the friend-making process, as well as the most difficult. For shy people, striking up conversation with a stranger or distant acquaintance causes great anxiety. Even socially comfortable people find it easier to talk with friends they know well rather than chat up new ones. In either instance, getting over your fears and being active rather than passive is key. You can't depend on the situation, another person, or fate to intervene and help things along. This is where letting your guard down is a must. What have you got to lose?

You'll need to ask a question or make a remark to get the conversation started—this is your "pick-up line." While "pick-up line" has a bad connotation—usually meaning a cheap, off-color comment made to seduce a person—the concept of "friend pick-up lines" doesn't have to.

The best kinds of questions or comments are those that require more than a yes or no answer or otherwise pave the way for follow-up conversation. Try complimenting something your potential friend is wearing, or asking her opinion on a current event, or focus on your surroundings for conversation topics. For example: "That is such a lovely necklace you're wearing. May I ask where you got it?"

If your antennae are up and you are sincere in your interest, your salutation will likely be well received. People are always flattered when you go out of your way to approach them and, even better, want to know their opinion on a subject. As a general rule, most people are usually more interested in talking about themselves than you would believe, too. It's often surprising how easy it is for people to engage in conversation. So, ask away!

"Which is the best of the local museums?"
"Have you read anything interesting lately?"
"Can you suggest a good movie to see with young kids?"

All these questions empower the recipient, imply your interest in what they have to say, and can lead to interesting conversation. Once you've made some headway with preliminary conversation, you can use the clues your antennae are receiving directly from the person to hone your questions. Further probing may reveal that this isn't actually someone you want to befriend, or, conversely, you may discover a true friend in the making. Either way, it's noble to have made the attempt. Time and time again, your gains will outweigh the duds.

☐ *Write down a list of five possible "friend pick-up lines,"*
i.e., conversation starters. Be brave and try them all out at the
next social function you attend.

MAKE EYE CONTACT

Have you ever been in a conversation with someone who refuses to look you in the eye? His or her gaze anxiously scans the room, leaving you with the unfortunate impression that there is either somewhere else this person would rather be or someone else this person would rather be speaking to. An equally uncomfortable (and strange) situation is when you're talking to someone who stares at any other part of your body—your shoulder, hair, or your cleavage—just to avoid looking you in the eye. And all this time, your mother told you that your eyes were your best feature!

Of course, we all know that a good conversation involves much more than simply talking. Body language is a necessary component of every conversation we have. The clarity of our look and the quality of our gaze—calm/intense or focused/distracted—speaks volumes about who we are, without one word of verbal communication being uttered.

So, with all this in mind, when you are introduced to someone, don't be afraid to look directly at him or her and to smile with your eyes. Your open attitude and willingness to meet new friends will be evident at first glance.

☐ *Have a conversation with an established friend
and ask him or her not to look at you as you speak. Repeat the
conversation but ask your friend to look you in the eyes.*

EAVESDROP (POLITELY, OF COURSE)

No, we don't want you to strain your neck while angling to get into the best eavesdropping position. We do, however, want you to pay close attention to the subtle tidbits of information people drop in casual conversation. There, we said it: we advocate eavesdropping (it's certainly better than name-dropping!) Why? It's a highly effective, quick way to get a "behind-the-scenes" sense of someone's personality and find a conversation starter; it's also a helpful method for you to hone your listening skills.

You must exhibit extreme finesse, however, while eavesdropping. If you can smell someone's perfume/cologne and make out the pores on their face, you are standing too close! Likewise, there are times when you should not intrude on an on-going discussion. If, for example, you happen to eavesdrop on a highly personal conversation, step back and give these people their space. Ask yourself this simple question: Would I want the input of a stranger at this time? If the answer is no, don't interrupt. However, if the conversation seems joinable, venture an opinion. "I saw that game, too—could you believe that call?"

☐ *Listen to the conversation around you and silently practice what you might say to the speakers.*

RULE #8

BE VULNERABLE

How often have you met someone who wouldn't let down his or her guard? The conversation stalls or becomes painfully awkward, punctuated with long, empty pauses and miserable attempts to resuscitate the connection: "It sure did rain a lot today, didn't it?" Here's a tip: showing your vulnerability will eventually break the ice, giving the most frigid conversationalist reason to warm to you and, in time, reveal his or her guarded personality.

A self-deprecating or revealing comment about yourself helps others to let their guard down—after all, you, not they, are in the spotlight. You might jokingly admit, "I'm so bad with names, I can hardly remember my own. Do you have a method for remembering them?" or come clean with, "This is my first time at this class, and I'm a little nervous." By admitting you don't know everything, you give others an opportunity to showcase their knowledge, which is guaranteed to make even the most socially guarded talkative. And you just might learn something new. With luck, you'll also gain a new friend. Not bad for a few minutes' worth of showing your belly. At the very least, it's better than talking about the rain.

☐ *Come up with a couple of slightly self-effacing remarks and, the next time a conversation stalls, use them.*

1. *Compliments: Everyone loves getting them. The key is to not be overly personal—it is fine to admire an item that a person is carrying or wearing, but not to comment on someone's looks or personality. For example, "I have been admiring your handbag. Where is it from?" or "What a great pair of sneakers."*

2. *Opinion Soliciting: People enjoy giving their opinions. Current events provide many openings. For example, "What do you think about the outcome of today's trial?"*

3. *Information Request: Who doesn't like to feel helpful? "What is a good local restaurant?" or "Can you suggest the best way to get to _____?"*

4. *Conversation Joining: This works best at a social gathering. Pick up on something the person has been saying or doing. For example, "I see you're drinking the specialty cocktail. Is it sweet?" or "I happened to hear your comment on the latest Star Wars movie, and I totally agree."*

5. *Provocation: This option requires a certain finesse to be amusing but not off-putting—you want to incite conversation not annoyance! For example, "Of the Seven Deadly Sins, which one do you think is least sinful?"*

THE PIANO MAN

In 1979, I read a new book by A. Scott Berg on Max Perkins. Barely a week after finishing the book, I went to the University of Colorado at Boulder, where I had been invited to participate in the Council on World Affairs, an organization founded by sociologist Howard Hickman in the late 1940s to stimulate intelligent conversation on important contemporary issues. Every year he gathered about fifty guests from a wide variety of disciplines and success levels for a week of panel discussions. That April, Daniel Ellsberg was the headliner, and he was joined by other luminaries, such as Lukas Foss, pianist and conductor; Pepper Schwartz, sociologist; Roger Ebert, film critic; Peter Davison, poet and director of the Atlantic Monthly Press; Frankie Hewitt, director of Ford's Theater; and Jack Nessel, editor of Psychology Today. My contribution would be to bring a retailer's perspective to the conference, and to talk about mail-order marketing, which was rather new at the time.

Convinced I wouldn't know anyone there, I dreaded the social awkwardness I was sure I'd feel at the welcome cocktail party. When I arrived, I noticed a piano in the corner of the room at which a young man was playing "Blah Blah Blah," an obscure Gershwin song. Being a Gershwin fan, I was familiar with the tune and intrigued that this piano player in Colorado—so far from the cabaret circuit—knew it, too. I became even more intrigued when the young man, who I had thought was the hired entertainment for the evening, got up from the piano and started to mingle with the guests. I approached him and asked about the Gershwin song. After a few minutes of conversation on the topic, he introduced himself, saying, "I'm Scott Berg."

I gushed like a starstruck groupie, telling him how great I thought his book was. It turned out that he was a huge fan of my mail-order catalog, The Horchow Collection. After our mutual fawning subsided, we resumed talking about our interest in Gershwin. It turned out that Scott had been using the piano as a retreat from conversation, a technique I sometimes resort to as well, so it was wonderful to have connected with each other on that level and so many others. For the rest of the week, we would find each other during lunch breaks and continue our conversation.

We have now been friends for almost thirty years—all because of a random meeting at what I had thought might be a boring conference. It ended up being the opposite—such a wonderful retreat from my everyday activity that I returned for three subsequent years and met many interesting people in fields I'd never before had contact with. If I had been more guarded—if I hadn't gone over to speak with the "piano player," or if I'd restrained myself from enthusing about his book—our meeting might have been just another "nice-to-meet-you" encounter. But because my antennae were up and I let my guard down, even at the risk of looking a bit foolish, my "Blah Blah Blah" led to a decades-long friendship that has been anything but blah!

RULE #9

BE "SET UP"

We've all heard the popular saying, "Birds of a feather flock together." It follows that your friends' friends are probably people that you will like, too. The Web site, www.friendster.com, was designed and built with this premise in mind. Think about it: in a world populated by billions and billions of people, your potential best friend could be separated from you by only six degrees! To test this theory, expand your own social circle by allowing people—even inviting them—to "set you up" with other potential friends.

We know, we know, you want to reject this method. It reeks of the last disastrous blind date you were set up on. We know that you might not like the idea that anyone—even your close friends—could truly "know" your taste in friends, or you might have an aversion to a meeting predicated only upon knowing someone in common. Why then (yes, we hear your screams and plaintive wails) are we such advocates? Allow us to explain:

Roger resisted Fred Smith's suggestion that he meet Fred's other friend, Michael Schaenen, for at least five years. Finally, when Roger and Mickey met by accident at a party in Dallas, they discussed how they hadn't wanted to be "set up" with each other, but nevertheless became fast friends—just like Fred said they would.

Sally did the same thing when her friend Keven McAlester suggested she might really like his college pal, Stephanie Furman.

After avoiding Keven's friendly suggestion for two years, Sally met Stephanie at a "game night" in San Francisco, and they've been friends ever since.

As these stories illustrate, you have nothing to lose by getting set up. The longer you wait, the less time you may have to enjoy a new friendship.

Set-ups are also great for meeting people in a new town or an unfamiliar situation. To avoid the potential awkwardness of a first meeting, ask an established friend of yours—whose taste and opinion you trust—invite both you and a potential friend to a social event. Better yet, take the bull by the horns: host your own party and ask everyone to bring someone that you don't know. This automatically expands your social circle for you and everyone else, too.

☐ *Host a party for your good friends and ask each of your guests to bring one person that you don't know.*

BE A RECEIVER

We hope that by now you see all the new opportunities for friendship in your life. It's entirely possible, too, that you have developed your conversational radar and are now capable of deciphering interesting discussions occurring two rooms away! You may even have offered a smile or a "hello" to someone you see regularly but don't know yet or have progressed to starting a conversation. How wonderful! But now it's time for you to step back and let the object of your attention respond.

To be an active participant in a conversation you must receive as well as give. Don't be so focused on your approach that you forget the goal: to get to know another person. A successful conversation, like a relationship, requires give and take—sometimes at the vigorous pace of a tennis volley and other times as leisurely as a waltz—and you should be attuned to this pattern.

Allow your conversational partner the opportunity to respond; look for ways to draw them into the dance. Do not come on too strong: if you are overly loquacious, argumentative, or revealing, you will end up creating resistance just when you want to lower it. Worst of all, if you don't stop and let him or her respond, you might discourage your new conversational partner all together.

□ *Let the other person talk.*

MAKE ROOM FOR NEW FRIENDS

Contrary to popular belief, a person's "friend capacity" is not finite. It is quite possible to make room in your life for additional friendships without sacrificing existing ones. All you need is the motivation. So good riddance to:

"My schedule/plate is full."
"I'm too shy."
"I hardly have time to keep up with my regular friends."
"I don't have the energy."

These excuses only rob you of the will to expand your circle of friends. Not every friendship has to be incredibly time-consuming: you can have fulfilling relationships with people you see infrequently as long as the contact you do have is meaningful. So if you feel like you are running out of friend "real estate," remember that being open to new friendships has no downside: it costs you nothing and can bring great rewards. And believe it or not, meeting new people will make you a better friend to the ones you already have!

☐ *Write down the excuses you employ to avoid meeting new friends in one column. In another column, write down the benefits of engaging new friends. Weigh the two columns.*

CHAPTER TWO

The Art of Listening

*It is the province of knowledge to speak,
and it is the privilege of wisdom to listen.*
—OLIVER WENDELL HOLMES, SR.

No one will be surprised to hear—pun intended—that being a good listener is tantamount to being a good friend. Not only is listening essential in the early stages of forming a connection, but it will also improve and enrich an already established relationship. Generally, we tend to think more about what we want to say next than about what is being said to us. If you want to be a good conversationalist, and by extension, friend, avoid this self-absorption trap and instead, learn to really listen. It may take you longer to formulate your response, but if you have really listened to your friend, you will surely say something more sensitive, intelligent, or appropriate in return!

LISTEN BEFORE YOU SPEAK

A real conversation cannot be one-sided. When talking with a friend, or potential friend, take the time to listen first, and worry later about being heard yourself. Your generosity will be reciprocated.

The foundation for a meaningful friendship, one that is based on mutual respect and caring, starts the moment you meet someone. At that point, you are presented not only with that person's words, but also with lots of other information: their tone of voice, body language, colloquialisms, and mannerisms. The way you absorb and respond to that wealth of information can make or break the new relationship. If someone senses that you are not making the effort to listen or are not really interested in what they are saying, they will probably just stop talking to you. But if you make an effort to genuinely hear and understand, you will generate further conversation—and a real connection. Listen up!

☐ *In your next conversation, note any tendency on your part to drift away while the other person is speaking, and focus your attention on their words.*

RULE #13

PRACTICE "ACTIVE" LISTENING

If you really attend to what you hear, chances are you will learn something new about the world around you. You may learn new information on a subject you thought you had understood perfectly. You may uncover a new insight into someone who interests you. People are like living, breathing books and at every turn, they can offer gifts of their own knowledge. Unfortunately, many people are not alert to this possibility, even with their closest friends.

Every individual you encounter has some knowledge or experience, on at least one subject, at the very least, that you have not. Remember this, and you will learn from the people that surround you—friends and strangers alike. If you listen well, think about what you hear, and apply your newfound knowledge, your day-to-day chats will improve and the overall quality of your friendships will deepen. Practicing active listening opens up a new world of potential relationships.

☐ *In each conversation, listen carefully and pick up at least one thing you did not know before.*

My friend Dick Bass (now into his seventies) has traveled far and wide and had many adventures. His achievements include being the first person to climb the highest peak on each of the seven continents, as well as being the oldest person (by five years) to climb Mount Everest (at the age of fifty-five.)

He once told me a story of a plane ride, on which he sat next to a nice man who listened to him go on about the treacherous peaks of Everest and McKinley, the time he almost died in the Himalayas, and his upcoming plan to reclimb Everest. Just before the plane landed, Bass turned to the man sitting next to him and said, "After all this, I don't think I've introduced myself. My name is Dick Bass." The man shook his hand, and responded, "Hi, I'm Neil Armstrong. Nice to meet you."

Just think of what Bass might have discovered had he stopped talking long enough to ask his traveling partner a question or two.

FOCUS ON THE SPECIFICS

People constantly pepper their stories with detailed descriptions or specific facts that are often buried by the larger, seemingly more important, aspects of a story. Sometimes, too, a person's larger-than-life personality can render the small details of a conversation seemingly inconsequential. Yet if you pay attention to the specifics of conversation, you may discover in them that you have things in common that could form an instant bond.

It's great to learn so quickly that someone's likes or dislikes may be similar to yours, and it's also helpful in moving along a friendship. "You mentioned you were biking last weekend," you might say to someone who talked about it in passing. "I love to mountain bike. Where do you go?"

In this brief interaction you can see precisely how drawing on the specifics of a conversation enables you to advance the relationship. First, you show that you were really listening: "You mentioned you were biking last weekend." Then you point out a common bond and offer positive reinforcement by saying, "I love to mountain bike." The final question is perhaps the most important because it leads to extended interaction: "Where do you ride?"

☐ *After meeting someone you would like to know better, write down as many things as you can remember about your conversation. The more specific, the better.*

THE FABRIC OF "FOUNDATIONAL" FRIENDSHIPS

I am on the board of the Committee for the Preservation of the White House, a non-political group that deals with the public rooms of the White House. At my first meeting, in the White House Family Dining Room, a long discussion ensued about replacing the draperies in the East Room. Mrs. Walter Annenberg, who had once been secretary of protocol for President Reagan, pointed out that Jacqueline Kennedy had ordered a double quantity of that particular fabric, which would enable the present curator to replace the draperies and restore the room to its past beauty.

I then listened with great interest as "Rusty" Powell, director of the National Gallery of Art, and Helen Cooper, curator of American paintings at Yale University Art Gallery, discussed the period furniture, color of the rooms, and placement of various works of art and decorative objects. Paying attention to what they were suggesting opened up a whole new area of dialogue for me and helped me expand my own knowledge immensely. I hadn't fully appreciated this new area of mutual interest until I listened.

FILE IMPORTANT FACTS

Remembering details that you learn about people in early meetings can serve to be a great friendship-building tool. If you can recall a remark made during a previous conversation, then refer to it the next time you are chatting, your potential friend will know you were interested enough to remember what she said. Similarly, if a colleague happens to mention an upcoming birthday, surprise him with a card. If a new neighbor comments on how much she loves tiramisu, invite her for tea and serve that special treat. The recipient of such thoughtfulness is sure to be flattered that you remembered.

This kind of careful listening is also useful in maintaining or deepening existing friendships. Imagine your friend's happiness when you send him a new book by an author he mentioned liking, or the warm reaction of a childhood pal when you remind her of times gone by with a box of Girl Scout cookies.

You might wonder how such attentiveness is possible. How can you be expected to remember the details of every conversation at every party? Of course, you can't and we don't expect you to. We advise keeping a friendship journal or calendar to record important dates and make notes. If you're more technologically proficient, put your PDA or BlackBerry to good use.

☐ *Get into the habit of noting people's likes in your address book or calendar.*

PERSONALIZE IT

In addition to remembering important details, events, or birthdays, you should look for unique ways to personalize your friendship. Instead of simply meeting a friend for lunch, make a more thoughtful, meaningful gesture. If, for example, you know that your friend loves the Kentucky Derby, why not invite her over for some mint juleps and friendly betting while you watch the race? Or, if an acquaintance has moved into a new apartment in your neighborhood, why not offer to show him around?

Most of us see these tasks as part and parcel of friendship, and they are. Taking the time to be thoughtful in this way is a way of expressing yourself. The point is to make the other person know that you care about them, and to do something about it. Correspondence and action—like compliments—mean much more when they are unexpected and supposedly unnecessary, and they give you an easy way to express your true feelings. This is how you can differentiate yourself as a friend before it's time to lend an ear at a serious juncture.

☐ *Make a list of your friends. Jot down several things you know each one likes. Randomly select a name and plan an activity for your friend based on that list.*

```
┌─────────────────────────────────┐
│                                 │
│   ┌─────────────────────────┐   │
│   │                         │   │
│   │      HORCHOW'S          │   │
│   │                         │   │
│   │   WEEKLY HALLMARK       │   │
│   │                         │   │
│   └─────────────────────────┘   │
│                                 │
└─────────────────────────────────┘
```

HORCHOW'S WEEKLY HALLMARK

Like many people, I like to leverage birthdays for keeping in touch. I stockpile cards throughout the year, buying them in advance whenever I see some that I like. I note birthdays on my monthly calendar, pocket calendar, and Palm Pilot to keep the birthdays of those I meet well organized. (Those who keep fewer than three calendars will find this task a little easier!)

At the beginning of each week, I send out that week's allotted birthday cards, taking time to write a thoughtful note in each. I also enjoy sending electronic cards because you can set them up months in advance to be e-mailed on the appropriate day. That way, there's no chance you'll forget a birthday.

YES, AND . . .

Sometimes even the most motivated conversationalists find themselves faltering. An infelicitous interruption, an inhibited partner,
or just an awkward moment can derail an exchange. How can you
nurture a failing conversation? Take a tip from improv. A useful
technique of improvisational comedy, is called "yes, and." It
means that no matter what someone says during a sketch, you
never deny the direction they are going. For example, "Alligator
wrangling ain't what it used to be," begets "Yes, and the quicksand
makes it all the more challenging." Even if you don't agree with
what someone is saying (or think is funny), "yes, and"-ing, helps
continue the improvisation, and, in life, the conversation. Like
the universally positive reaction to a smile, "yes, and"-ing makes
people feel good.

For example, if someone says, "I am amazed at how blue the
ocean is in this part of the country," a "yes, and" response might
be, "Yes, and the beaches are large as well." A contrary response
might be, "I've seen bluer." The first response encourages conversation to continue, giving you the chance to steer it in a more
appealing direction; the other stops it in its tracks.

☐ *Play this improv game with friends. One person makes a silly statement. The
next person replies with "yes, and" and adds a new bit of information to the
statement. Keep going until you run out of details to add (which may be impossible).*

RULE #18

YES, BUT . . .

Although honesty and healthy debate are vital and important aspects of real communication, there are times when confrontation is unwelcome, and you would rather avoid the train wreck of an unnecessary altercation. When you see the steam engine barreling toward you, get off the tracks and end the conversation. We know, though, that there are times when escape isn't possible and you feel as though you've been tied to the tracks with heavy-duty rope. Try using the "yes, but" technique. It will allow you to diffuse the disaster without compromising your beliefs.

Politely acknowledge that you have heard what someone has said but that you disagree with him or her. "Yes, but I'm afraid I don't quite see it that way." If both parties are listening thoughtfully, you each may gain perspective on how the other person thinks. If you find, however, that the person you are speaking to refuses to listen to your point of view, do your best to derail the arguer by agreeing to disagree. If all else fails, excuse yourself to go to the restroom.

☐ *Practice your exit strategy with a close friend.*

Once I found myself on the other end of a very derisive rant by Mr. X, a notoriously prejudiced man who happens to be the chairman and former director of a family owned, world-famous company. Instead of responding with my true feelings to Mr. X's decidedly contemptuous remarks, I guardedly commented, "Oh, really?" or "You don't mean it?" Even though I disagreed in the extreme to what was being said, I also wanted to avoid an awkward and loaded confrontation in an otherwise very polite and enjoyable social gathering.

At the end of the evening, Mr. X said, "That Horchow is a chip off the old block. I really enjoyed meeting him." Because I had held my tongue, Mr. X erroneously believed that we had made some kind of connection. If Mr. X had really been listening, however, he would have noticed that I was neither agreeing nor connecting with him but was, instead, tactfully maneuvering my way around having to engage in an unwanted debate.

Evaluate the Candidate

This may sound more like advice for interviewing a job applicant, but it does apply. Once you have gotten past the initial phase of getting to know someone, it's time to evaluate. Pay attention to your instincts. Listen for clues that will help you gauge the potential of a friendship so you can bypass unnecessary future conflicts and toxic connections for fruitful, healthy ones.

Of course, negative conversational clues don't always preclude you from pursuing a friendship. But they can inform your future relations with the person by helping you identify early on what issues will be conflictual or harmonious, or how you can and will relate to each other.

For example, a person may make it clear in the early stages of a relationship that he or she is most comfortable when "helping" or serving a purpose. If your relationship should change someday, so you are no longer the person "in need," this friend may not be as interested in keeping up ties. On the flip side, recognizing that someone is engaging, interested, and enthusiastic during your initial conversations is probably a good indication of positive future interaction, and a clue that the person may be willing and able to have a more intimate friendship with you in the future.

☐ *Be aware of "warning signs" (see page 44)*
that indicate a possibly bad friendship match.

A LESSON IN LENOX

When I was a young buyer in Houston at Foley's Department Store, I became friendly with the Lenox china salesman. Foley's was the largest buyer of Lenox in Texas, and when the sales representative visited Houston, he always took me out to dinner. Over time, we became very good friends. I believed that our friendship had transcended the buyer-salesman relationship.

When I moved to Dallas to Neiman Marcus, the store did not sell Lenox china. Even though my good friend the sales rep lived in nearby Fort Worth, I never heard from him—not a word. I was very disappointed, but I learned a good lesson.

Years later, when I was selecting merchandise for The Horchow Collection, I visited a showroom where I was greeted effusively by—guess who? My "friend," who was now in the giftware business (and hoping to sell to my catalog). He quickly reminded me of our long "friendship," and I took some pleasure in remarking that there had certainly been a long time in between visits for two people who lived only forty minutes apart.

EARLY WARNING SIGNS

Consider these warning signs reasons to be cautious in proceeding with a relationship:

1. *Someone who tells lies or cheats with ease. A person who is comfortable with dishonesty is likely to lie to you, too.*
2. *Someone who criticizes others. You never know when your friendship might fall out of favor, and your flaws become a discussion topic for this person.*
3. *Someone who brags about getting away with things. That person might decide to put something over on you one day.*
4. *Someone who is openly argumentative or combative. Who needs it?*
5. *Someone who is a "victim" or collects injustices. These folks are never satisfied with the way they are treated—even by you.*
6. *Someone who offers too much information too early. People who tell you their personal business very quickly often tend to become overly reliant or needy.*
7. *Someone who makes empty promises. You don't need an unreliable friend in your life.*
8. *Someone who refuses to look you in the eye. If someone is constantly looking for someone "better" to talk to, you should move on.*

ADVANCED LISTENING: BUILD TRUST

Perhaps the most important component of friendship is trust. Without it, there can be no real confidence in the relationship, and no room for growth beyond the superficial. Building trust requires a leap of faith (or a series of small leaps) but you'll find it worth the risk.

Let your friends know that you accept them just as they are, that you will not reject them despite the occasional failing. Then trust that they will do the same for you. (One of the great rewards of friendship is that it gives you the opportunity to work through your flaws in a safe way with people who love and respect you.)

Keep your friends' best interests at heart, and know that they are looking out for yours. The good turns you do for them will come back to you.

Keep your friends' secrets, and they will keep yours.

Finally, freely express your regard and affection for your friends, and accept theirs in return. The more you give, the more you are likely to receive.

☐ *Entrust a friend with a secret about yourself.*

FIND THE BALANCE

In a healthy friendship, the give-and-take of listening is balanced. Day-to-day exchanges are equally about each other's experiences and feelings. When you have a more serious need to talk, your friend will happily take on the listening role, knowing that when she has a problem, you will be all ears. Roger's friend Jacques has an amusing take on this aspect of their relationship: at the beginning of their weekly lunch, he asks, "Do you want to be the baby today? Or do you want to be the father?"

You may not discuss the balance as openly, but you should be aware of it—and avoid letting it tilt too far in one direction. Being a good listener does not mean that all you do is listen; it means that you respond sensitively, and share your own relevant experiences. A relationship in which one person does all the talking and the other all the listening is a shrink-patient relationship, not a friendship!

☐ *Make sure there is an even exchange of listening and speaking in your next conversation with a good friend. If it's all about you, fix the imbalance.*

EMPATHIZE

A good friend offers empathy but is cautious with advice. No matter how close your friendship, be careful about giving counsel. When a friend tells you a deep, dark secret from her childhood or confides an intimate detail of her marriage, even if it seems she wants more from you than to lend a non-judgmental ear, for the sake of your future bond, leave advice-giving to the professionals and offer empathy instead.

This may seem like withholding, but, in fact, empathy has a lot to offer: showing that you really understand how it feels to be sad, ashamed, or in pain helps the sufferer to feel less alone. When you empathize with a friend's predicament you show that you care and provide solace for your friend's woes. And when you have a problem, sharing it with a friend eases the burden.

Advice-giving, on the other hand, though well-intended, poses some difficulties. If your friend takes your suggestions, but the outcome isn't positive, both of you will feel uncomfortable. If your advice is ignored, however, you may find yourself feeling somewhat offended. The best advice? Let your friends know you are always there to listen, and if real advice is required, share the name of your therapist.

☐ *The next time a friend brings you her woes, resist the urge to tell her what to do; instead, show her that you understand how she feels.*

CHAPTER THREE

The Art of
Genuine Conversation

Do not save your loving speeches
For your friends till they are dead;
Do not write them on their tombstones,
Speak them rather now instead

—ANNA CUMMINS

Friendship cannot be built on small talk alone. Yes, there is a time and a place for it, but it isn't the heart of a true connection—genuine conversation is. Think about it: without interesting, inspiring conversation, life would be about as dull as the weather you'd be forced to talk about. So, move beyond the meaningless patter of the initial greeting, and make a sincere attempt to talk about things that are a meaningful. It may be just the jolt of lightning needed to spark a true friendship.

REMEMBER NAMES
(AND OFFER YOUR OWN)

Before conversation gets going—small talk or otherwise—we introduce ourselves to people and exchange names. Remembering the name of the person you meet sets the stage for a possible friendship. Many times we are so preoccupied with what's going on around us at the moment of the introduction that we immediately forget the name of the person we've just met. Other times we subconsciously think we'll never see the person again or have reason to talk to him, and thus, the name goes in one ear and out the other!

If you are interested in meeting people and having meaningful relationships, it is important to focus on the moment of introduction and remember the name of the person you are being introduced to. This will lead to a more in-depth, personal interaction thereafter, and it sends a message to the person that you are interested in getting to know her.

Of course, this is much easier said than done. Most people aren't good with names. So, don't worry—it's inevitable that a name will occasionally slip away from you. When the conversation is more memorable than the name, admit that you've forgotten the person's name but say that you do remember the great conversation you had about women in politics or making sushi. Most of the time, people will forgive your forgetfulness. If you think someone might really be offended, however, surreptitiously ask someone else to jog your memory of that person's name when they're out of earshot. Say, "Nice to see you" rather than "Nice to meet you." No one wants to think they were so completely forgettable that you've blanked out the first meeting.

Usually, honesty is the best policy. Say, "I'm terrible with names," introduce yourself again, and then buy a memory book and get to work! If a memory book doesn't strike your fancy, there are scores of other ways to overcome this hurdle, from memorization games to hypnosis. Mostly, though, it just takes focus and a sincere interest to remember someone's name.

Do what you can to end the widespread name-forgetting epidemic. If you have the chance to do so, mention people by name as much as possible to others. When you introduce people to each other, follow up with each party the next time you see them and remind them of the people they met. Help people remember your name by spelling it for them or creating a pneumonic device for them, like a rhyming poem. When Roger was a freshman at Yale, for example, he ran for Student Council on the platform, "More Chow with Horchow." Even though he didn't win the election, you better believe his classmates remembered his name!

☐ *Come up with your own trick*
to help people remember your name.

RULE #24

MINIMIZE SMALL TALK

For every social situation, there is requisite small talk. It consists of questions that everyone comes prepared to ask and answer, uncontroversial observations, and topics that are familiar. It's totally predictable and sometimes amusing, and serves the purpose of putting people at ease.

As small talk cynics, we're often tempted to throw off the equilibrium by answering these questions with sarcasm, or some other startling response. However when people ask, "How are you?" they usually don't want to hear, "Okay. If only I could just get rid of this darn groin pain," or "Great, except that I lost my cat."

"Fine," in this case, is absolutely fine; small talk is expected and required in certain situations. However, too often it is used as a shield, and keeps people from really getting to know each other better. The key is to know how to use it productively and how to avoid using it as a crutch.

Take as your rule of thumb: only one small-talk question and response is allowed. Then you must move on to more meaningful, specific talk.

☐ *Write down five thought-provoking questions to ask as soon as the small talk is over.*

BANISH THE BANALITIES

The following five questions and their many variations are guaranteed to get you nowhere in a conversation:

1. *Unless you are seriously inquiring into the state of someone's health, "How are you?" is not an effective conversation starter.*
2. *We all live by the same calendar, and it's no great surprise when Friday turns into the weekend. You may, however, ask for more details about someone's weekend to start a real conversation.*
3. *At a wedding, dozens of well-meaning people will surely ask the bride and groom: "Where are you honeymooning?" Every pregnant woman tires of answering "When are you due?" Think of questions that don't state the obvious.*
4. *Using a sports cliché is a time-honored conversational opener but it can be risky. You might encounter an avid fan unable to change the subject.*
5. *Unless you are a meteorologist or a farmer, there is usually nothing vitally interesting in a discussion of the weather.*

These small talk openers are nearly unavoidable in everyday interactions, but try to move beyond them quickly. Your goal is to learn about the person you are talking to, not make empty noise.

Start with Questions

When you first meet someone, you're both assessing whether you would be interested in further conversation. It's okay to use small talk to help you figure out if you want to ease into a more in-depth conversation. Ask questions that are specific to the situation to draw the other person out and try to stay on topic. If you're at a party, you might ask how the person knows the host, or what he or she thinks of the hors d'oeuvres. At a cultural event, you might ask the person what attracted her to the event. Topics that relate to the event allow you to probe without being inappropriate, but any topic that allows a person to reveal a little about himself is a good one.

When you offer your opinion about something, you reveal yourself. This kind of vulnerability leads to an exchange, and showing enthusiasm on a topic can be contagious. The light level of the conversation will allow the revelations to emerge at a comfortable pace. However, the old adage about avoiding politics or religion is apt—start with more neutral or universal topics when testing the waters with someone.

☐ *The next time you meet someone new, ask various event-related questions and see if you can guess where he or she is from.*

Use Small Talk Strategically

Be wary of lazy conversational gambits that may fill awkward spaces or transitions but don't really mean anything. A typical small-talk phrase such as, "Let's get together" (though you really have no interest in doing so) is often used when you just don't know what else to say. Unfortunately, if you say this when you don't mean it, you will be seen as insincere at best and dishonest at worst.

When you need to smooth over awkward moments, small talk is actually useful. Just as "transitional" small talk can move a conversation from opening superficialities to deeper levels, two other kinds of small talk can be useful:

"Maintenance" small talk: Use this when you want to maintain the status quo in a relationship or to downgrade a conversation to a more superficial level. Choose topics you both agree on or uncontroversial current events. Keep it light; be ready to move to "exit" small talk.

"Exit" small talk: Use this to escape a conversation entirely. Tell the person that you enjoyed chatting but must now be off (to an appointment, to the restroom, to make a call—you get the idea.)

If you are aware of these scenarios, you can use small talk in the way it was intended—to make people feel comfortable—and save yourself for more genuine conversations with someone else.

☐ *Pick a neutral topic to use for strategic small talk.*

Some years ago I found myself somewhat nervously using small talk to further along conversation with Glenn Close at a summer dinner party in Nantucket.

After I had been peppering her with an incessant drone of obvious questions—"How did you get into the acting world?" "Where are you from?" "Where did you go to school?"—Glenn finally suggested we might "dispense with the small talk" and get to know each other a little better.

Among other questions she asked me, a difficult one for me to answer was, "What were you like when you were in college?" I stammered and stuttered, which I don't normally do, and finally said that I guessed you might have called me, well, a nerd. She graciously said she didn't really believe that. A few minutes later we were walking along the wharf near the restaurant where we had dined, and she disappeared into a store, only to return with a box of Nerd Candy, which she presented to me. I took it home and it was the best joke on Dad of the summer. The children loved it.

If you can avoid unnecessary small talk and ask questions that require some thought, you will draw people out more easily. You'll find out a lot more about them and—who knows?—you might make a new friend.

PEEL BACK THE ONION

Once you have met and had enough of an exchange to know that you're interested in a person, your conversation needs to develop beyond the superficial. If you use these moments together to reveal more about yourself and to discover more about the other person, you will be well on your way to a friendship.

It's important to be sensitive to where the conversation is leading, to gauge the person's relative interest, and find topics that further your interaction without getting too deeply personal. You don't have to answer "how are you" with any mind-boggling revelation about yourself. Nor should you meet someone and then immediately ask him or her, "Is your life happy?" Go a little deeper into basic topics, for example, "What do you enjoy most about your job?" and talk about things that you care about. If the conversation is memorable, it will lead to another one.

The second and third time you meet someone, you can reduce the amount of small talk. Open with a reminder of something you discussed or something that happened the last time you met in order to reacquaint yourself with the person, bring the conversation up to date, and make all parties comfortable. "The last time we met, we were talking about documentaries," you could say, following up with, "Did you have a chance to see any of the Oscar contenders?" Or: "Our last conversation about China was so interesting that I bought a book on it. Have you read it?"

Sometimes friendships linger a while in the small-talk transition level, depending on personalities, until you and your future friend feel more comfortable sharing with each other. As in studying, it might help to review the first chapter of your acquaintance before moving onto the next, so you should feel free to catch up using small talk, and then progress to genuine conversation.

This is the crucial moment when you leave behind transitional small talk for meaningful conversation. Now is the time to open subjects that explore more of your commonalities, reveal more about yourselves, and help you understand each other better. Now that you have some clues about the other person's interests, you should move the conversation to the next level and "peel back the onion."

If you're really lucky, you won't have to venture through any of the re-cap, review, and get-things-up-to-date small-talk moments at all. In ideal circumstances, which are largely dependent on intuition and mutual interest, you can skip small talk altogether—from as early as the first meeting—and get tight to the heart of the onion.

□ *Tell one revealing fact or story about yourself to a potential friend and see where it takes you.*

Make Your Conversations Count

The art of conversation is really the skill of being able to listen well and to respond in a way that deepens the interaction. If you have been practicing your listening techniques and have mastered the uses of small talk, you are ready to begin enjoying meaningful conversations with friends new and old.

What makes a discussion meaningful? It may vary a little from person to person but there are a few elements common to pretty much every truly significant talk:

- It should occur at a time and place where you can both focus on the interaction. This could be a dinner party but probably not at a disco.

- It has to be about something that matters to you. This doesn't mean the conversation has to be serious or grave, just that you should care about the subject you're discussing. Obvious topics include family, career, beliefs, and goals, but any topic that means something to you is fine—from love, death, and taxes to your lifelong love of African violets. At this level of conversation, the proscription against religion and politics no longer holds—have at it!

- It requires each participant to reveal something of themselves. Unless you are honestly expressing how you feel or what you truly think about the subject, the conversation won't progress beyond the superficial. Remember: a true friendship is one based on meaningful connection.

- It's okay to be emotional. When something really matters to you, it is not unusual for talking about it to make you feel excited, happy, sad, or even angry. If these emotions are coming out in your conversation, remember that it is the subject, not the person you are talking to, that makes you feel this way. If your friend is an old pal, an emotional discussion will feel natural. If you are getting to know a new friend, it may feel a little awkward—if you are not ready to go there with each other, lighten up, knowing that you can revisit the topic as your mutual trust grows.

☐ *Make the subject of your next social conversation something you really care about.*

CHAPTER FOUR

Expand Your Circle

Fate chooses your relations,
you choose your friends.
—JACQUES DELILLE

If you always order crème brûlée, how will you ever discover your love for cannoli? The world is only as large (and delicious!) or as small as you make it. Meeting new people and developing new friendships is invariably life-enhancing, and you're never too old to start. Don't miss out by rigidly sticking to your existing social circle. Stay open to the idea that you can find new friends at every stage of life. The simplest way to do it is to break out of your regular routine. Go on. Don't be afraid. Take a big bite and savor each and every one of your new adventures.

ALTER YOUR ATTITUDE

Deciding to put yourself in situations—physically and emotionally—that are different from your norm is the best way to prepare yourself to meet new people. You will get a new perspective on life simply by being willing to interact with people you normally wouldn't. Challenging yourself to try something new—even if it's as simple as walking a new way to work or trying a different table in the commissary—could immediately put you in contact with someone you've never met, which could lead you to a completely new group of friends and possibly a new life! That may sound extreme, but it's completely possible. We have a friend who took our advice once and while spending one afternoon at a new dog park with his mutt, he met the woman he ended up marrying.

If you are willing to step outside your comfort zone, you'll find a whole new world of opportunities awaiting you. But you have to believe that expanding your circle, casting a wider net, kissing a lot of frogs—or whatever metaphor you like—will more lead to good things.

☐ *Go somewhere new, scan the setting for a potential friend, and say hello.*

CHANGE YOUR DAY-TO-DAY HABITS

We all have regular routines we follow and ingrained patterns of behavior. Here are some suggestions for changing your day-to-day habits to allow for more spontaneous (and fun) meetings:

- Take time with breakfast instead of rushing. Stop at a different coffee shop. Instead of sitting hunched over your coffee reading the newspaper, make a point of saying hello to one person.

- Lunch is the perfect time of day to take a break from your routine. Pack a lunch and go to a local park to eat it. Enjoy the noontime sun and be open to connections.

- Dinner (or cocktail hour) is the most popular time to get together with friends. Shake up the routine and try a new restaurant or bar. Organize a cocktail party and invite a new acquaintance.

- Although the shortest distance between two points is a straight line, it can also be the least interesting route. Try a different path or vary your mode of transportation.

- If you might have fallen into the habit of watching television or reading a book to unwind, instead consider a visit your local bookstore to browse, or find a comfortable park bench and watch the sunset instead of TV.

- Answering your daily quota of e-mails can be more than simple routine. Take this opportunity to reconnect by sending a message to a friend you have lost touch with. Even better, handwrite a card and send it the old-fashioned way.

- If you like to read, join a book club.

- If you're normally a homebody who rents movies, invite some acquaintances over for a movie night.

- The people who live in your neighborhood, condo, or building already share something in common with you. Introduce yourself: many lasting friendships have been formed over the backyard fence or in the apartment building foyer.

- Your work brings you in contact with a multitude of people. Instead of a quick nod, take the time for an introduction that might lead to a meaningful connection.

- Make a plan to meet in person a work colleague you know only through the phone or e-mail.

Stepping outside your comfortable boundaries might cause an edge of trepidation or nervousness. Accept the challenge! With each new encounter, the next becomes easier.

☐ *Try any one of the suggestions above.*

$$\boxed{\text{RULE} \mid \text{\#}31}$$

JOIN!

Variety, as the saying goes, is the spice of life. Most people, however, are pretty uncomfortable moving out of their regular trajectories if they don't have to—the very thought of meeting new people or changing comfortable habits can seem just plain inconvenient—or worse, scary. If the thought of straying from your daily path is akin to jumping headfirst into freezing cold water, we have a solution: join a pre-organized group of people that shares one (or more!) of your interests. With the initial what-are-we-going-to-talk-about stress neatly tied into the reason for meeting, you can relax, observe, and interact with others as you become comfortable. After that, making friends is inevitable.

To join a group or sign up for a class, simply think of the activities you already enjoy doing or, if you're feeling ambitious, activities you've always wanted to do but, for one reason or another, never have, like sky-diving, writing the Great American Novel, or running a marathon. You don't have to conquer the world (or win a Pulitzer)—sometimes trying something new can be as simple as bird-watching, learning how to knit, or, in Sally's case, making the perfect Thanksgiving turkey.

When Sally signed up for a cooking class at Sur la Table, not only did her bird come out just right, so did her new friendship with a fellow foodie. Neither went to the cooking class looking to meet someone new, but it was an unadvertised bonus to have done so. Roger experienced similar good fortune when he attended an intensive Spanish course at Dartmouth College one summer with Sally's sister, Lizzie. Besides learning how to habla Español, he met Congressman Pete Guerin, III, tambien.

Classes and groups, whether they are centered around doing something athletic, charitable, artistic, or political, don't have to require a long-term commitment and can be as passive as watching your favorite noir films or listening to original recordings of big band music. You may even want to join a class to get over a particular phobia. If you have a fear of water, for example, take a beginner's swimming class. We promise that once you get your toes wet, you'll be ready for the diving board in no time.

☐ *Sign up for a class or group-related activity.*

In 1955, I was a young man working in the basement of Foley's in Houston, ironing curtains and learning the retail ropes. My college roommates—Mike Egan, Wes Dixon, and Dick Grave—suggested that we all rendezvous in New Haven for our fifth reunion. It cost a lot of money to travel that far from Houston, and I wasn't very anxious to use my modest retail salary to do so; I kept up with all of the college friends I cared about and I could see my roommates any time. But the roommates were very persuasive, as friends can be at that age, and the next thing I knew I was on a plane back to the East Coast. It turned out to be one of the best things I ever did.

Although my college years were rewarding for me, there were many people in my class that I never met during the course of my years there. We had the largest class ever to graduate from Yale due to the end of World War II and the return of all the veterans. At the reunion, I met Bob Massie, an author who went on to write several books and win the Pulitzer Prize for Nicholas and Alexandra. In the relaxed atmosphere of the reunion, Bob and I had a long conversation about the meaning of friendship. We had our own for fifty years to follow. I also met Larry McQuade, who I had heard of in school. He played on the football team, was Phi Beta Kappa and a Rhodes Scholar—all things I wished I had accomplished, except for the football!—I never thought we would have anything in common. As it turns out, we enjoyed the pleasure of each other's company, and he remains one of my best friends.

Every encounter at my reunions hasn't been so pleasant; I have often been disappointed to find that the people who were jerks in high school were still jerks years later. They just turned into stockbroker jerks or lawyer jerks. One guy who had been a cocky, know-it-all shot putter on the high school track team was still a cocky know-it-all, but at the reunion, he insisted on trying to sell me life insurance. And I was single! I didn't need life insurance! However, meeting Bob Massie and Larry McQuade and all the other new friends I've met at reunions has kept me going back every chance I get. It's great to know that I will have at least one thing in common with every person there, but I often end up having much more in common than that with a few, jerks notwithstanding.

GET A GROUP

If you can't find a pre-established group that directly appeals to you, take matters into your own hands and start your own. Here are some examples:

- *Astronomy Group:* Members bring their own telescopes and stargaze.

- *Investing Club:* Members review investment planning strategies.

- *Cooking Club:* Members plan ethnic menus and everyone contributes one homemade dish.

- *Foreign-Language Table:* Members meet to practice their French (or Spanish, Chinese, Italian, etc.).

- *Gallery Group:* Members visit art galleries and discuss opinions over dinner.

- *Patent-Pending Group:* Members build various inventions and showcase them to one another.

- *Yoga and/or Pilates Group:* Members pay a monthly fee for instructors to teach intimate classes in their homes.

- *New Parents' Group:* Members meet to discuss the challenges of having a new baby.

☐ *Start your own activity-oriented group.*

SMALL TALK
WITH BIG PEOPLE

My sister Regen wished that more enlightening speakers would come to Dallas. Believing that she wasn't the only person in Dallas who felt that way, she started a lecture group called the Institute for Interesting People, invited speakers to come, and found many other people were just as interested as she was in hearing them. The speakers have included best-selling authors, Hollywood producers, and political activists. The now 350-member group assembles once every few months for a mid-day casual box lunch and a forty-five-minute talk, followed by a short reception or round-table discussion. That reception has sparked untold numbers of friendships, e-mail exchanges, and idea forums. And for Regen, it's also meant a whole new variety of people in her life.

TRAVEL

You probably already know that traveling is a mind-opening experience—why not make it a friend-expanding experience as well? It doesn't matter whether you are taking a trip across town or around the world; the experience of being somewhere new, where you don't know anyone and your usual habits don't apply, sets you up for new adventures. You'll find yourself more open to talking to strangers, so make the most of it. Or use the trip as an opportunity to strengthen an existing friendship. Here are some tips for making connections while you're on the go:

- *Meet the locals.* With help from a native, you will discover more about a new place than you could on your own, and you will have the opportunity to make a new friend. Connecting with someone whose background is different from your own is eye-opening, and may result in a relationship quite unlike those you already have back home.

- *Talk to other travelers.* As fellow visitors to someplace new, you already have something in common! Let that be a bridge to getting to know people.

- *Host foreign visitors.* Return the favor for someone you met abroad or offer to host visitors through an exchange service. Either way, your generosity will lead to new friendships—

and the experience of showing off your own home territory will lead you to appreciate it anew.

- *Travel with old friends.* "Togethering," or taking a trip with friends you haven't seen in a while, is the newest trend in travel. Rent a big house somewhere, grab some old school-mates, work pals, or childhood buddies, and spend a weekend doing something fun—and most important—catching up with each other.

- *Travel afar with someone near.* Taking a trip with someone you know is a great way to add a new dimension to your relationship. Taking the friendship out of its usual context and experiencing something new together will create fresh memories to cherish and build upon when you get back home.

☐ *Plan one trip to take this season, and come home with a new connection—then keep it up by e-mailing or sending a note.*

DON'T NEST, HIVE!

Have you ever looked closely at a beehive? And, no, we're not talking about the 1960s hairdo (although that, too, is awe-inspiring.) Linking together several intricately designed honey-combs, the beehive literally buzzes with social activity. If you think of your social circle as a hive, with potential to grow exponentially, your ability to make new friends (and connect them with already established ones) will be vastly enhanced.

In the late 1980s and early 1990s, trend forecaster Faith Popcorn was well known for coining the sociological concept of "nesting." She described it as people preferring to stay home to "cocoon" away from others, seeking refuge inside their familiar circle. Today, however, according to to Yankelovich, a Chapel Hill, NC-based marketing consultancy that tracks consumer attitudes, people are connecting with each other through the home by "hiving," In Sally's work as a lifestyle writer and through her entertaining at home, she has found that "hiving," or inviting people over to engage in group activities, is an easy way for people to form new and meaningful connections to each other. So, take a chance. Instead of staying safely cocooned in your nest, create a hive!

☐ *Expand your social circle by inviting your friends*
to bring new friends over for a group activity.

HIVE A LITTLE!

Any of the following are fun activities to invite people for:

• *Poker Night: Organize a poker night and ask a couple of friends to each bring someone you don't know well. You'll have a full house of new friends!*

• *Game Night: Cards may not be your thing, but almost everyone likes to play some kind of game, and it is a terrific way to learn about people. Try inviting a group over to play charades, a board game, a trivia challenge, or even musical chairs.*

• *Pot Luck Hors d'Oeuvres Party: When guests arrive, take a Polaroid of the guest with his/her creation and make a sign attributing each item to its creator. Then watch as people interact, share their favorites, give credit to each other, and learn more about each other.*

• *Monthly Salon: Pick a different topic to discuss each month depending on your groups' interest level.*

• *Scavenger Hunt: Create a list with point values for various free or easily attainable items, separate people into mixed groups, and give them two hours to collect what they can.*

EMPHASIZE QUALITY, NOT QUANTITY

With so many potential friends, it's tempting to load your Rolodex with name after name and collect phone numbers the same way Trump makes money—fast and furiously. Calm down and take a deep breath.

While there is always room in your life for one more friend (or two or three), do not rush the process and mistake the quantity of your friends for quality. Don't get us wrong: having a large number of diverse, interesting people peppering your life is a wonderful, life-improving thing. It's also possible to maintain many close relationships. But the goal in friendship should be to enjoy really knowing one another. You can only do that if you spend time together. So leave room in your life to engage in one-on-one activities with people whose friendship is important to you.

☐ *Spend some quality-time with a friend you haven't seen in awhile.*

$$\boxed{\text{RULE} \mid \#36}$$

USE TECHNOLOGY TO RE-CONNECT

Besides the big, beautiful world that lurks beyond your back-yard, there is another world—albeit a virtual one—hiding inside your computer. If you're still using the White Pages to locate long-lost friends, it's time to step into the Information Era. The World Wide Web is the final frontier for "branching out," providing unlimited ways for people to get to know each other, find commonalities, and connect. Social networks, urban tribes, and hiving are just a few of the people-based phenomena sprung from people-connecting Web sites like Friendster, Classmates, Match, Craig's List, and LiveJournal. The possibilities beyond chat rooms, user forums, and mobile phone text messaging are limitless.

Whenever Roger starts to wonder whatever happened to good friends from the past, whether that's childhood, the army, or high school, he searches for them by entering a name in Google, AnyWho, or one of the other "people-finder" Web sites.

It isn't always easy to find a childhood friend from seventy-three years ago, but he's done it—miraculously—courtesy of the Internet. Recently, Roger found his oldest friend Jay ("Jayboy") Eckert in Cincinnati, where he was born. Jay led him to his other old friend Bobby Hunsicker, who Jay knew had moved to Indiana. Roger sent old childhood pictures to them, bringing back all sorts of memories. Since Roger's children had no idea who those photos were of, and why he had them, it was great to be able to find the people who appreciated seeing themselves from so long ago.

Now that Jayboy, Bob, and Roger have all been in touch by e-mail, letter, and telephone, they are planning a wonderful reunion dinner. They've already been quizzing each other on how many neighbors' names they can remember from when they were kids! Without technology—in this case e-mail and search engines—Roger would never have had this extra dividend of friendship.

One caveat: while technology offers easy ways to connect with people, it can also keep people from doing the things that make relationships real and sustainable, like meeting and getting to know each other in person. It's important to use every means you can to reach out. Take advantage of the excellent ways the Internet has improved connectivity—but don't experience the world exclusively through your computer screen—friendships require in-person, face-to-face interaction (at least every once in awhile) to truly thrive.

☐ *Register yourself on a Web site that allows
you to network with other people.*

FRIENDLY TECHNOLOGY

Computer technology offers a host of resources to help you find and manage friendships.

- *Search Engines: These can help you locate people with whom you have lost touch but would like to reconnect. Three to try: Google.com, Yahoo.com, and AnyWho.com.*
- *Special-Interest Sites: If you love origami and would like to connect with other paper-folders, search the Web for "origami group" and you'll soon be trading folds. Meetup.com is a site that helps people with shared interests form groups.*
- *Bulletin Boards and Message Forums: There are many local web communities that list activities around town, including Craigslist.org and Citysearch.com.*
- *Social Networking Sites: These are Web sites that help you find new people who are also interested in expanding their social circles. Try Friendster.com.*
- *Party Organizers: These are Web sites that make it easy to hold a gathering by sending invitations, organizing replies, and sending reminders. Evite.com is one to try.*

CHAPTER FIVE

Follow-Up

Wishing to be friends is quick work,
but friendship is a slow-ripening fruit.

—ARISTOTLE

There's good reason that the term "budding" is often attached to friendship. Like planting a seed, friendship requires regular attention if it is to blossom and flourish. The fertilizer for successful friendships is the act of following up. Following up is the opposite of passively sitting back and waiting for friendships to occur; it's about making friendships a priority in your life and taking action to further enhance and improve them. Although this does take effort, the good news is that it is much easier, takes less exertion, and pays richer dividends than any other effort we can think of.

FOLLOW-UP,
FOLLOW-UP, FOLLOW-UP

For most people, the term "follow-up" is associated with business dealings. It's something to do after a job interview or an important meeting. Yet it should be an equally significant element of your personal life, for it is the single most important thing you can do to build friendships.

Applied to friendship, following up is not about making or breaking a deal. It is a way to show appreciation for another person, to express interest in getting to know them better, or simply to further a sense of connection. That's it. There is no obligation, no ulterior motive, no expectation of return on investment. Yet if you follow-up with friends as efficiently as you do in business, you will certainly reap countless benefits.

Following up in friendships requires that you get in touch with the person—by means of a phone call, note, or even a one-line e-mail—thereby letting them know that the relationship is important to you. It feels good and is almost always deeply appreciated. After all, when was the last time you didn't like it when someone thanked you? There is almost nothing better in the world than to receive unsolicited appreciation, praise, or friendly contact—except perhaps to send it to someone you care about.

☐ *Make a friendly "check-in" call with a friend you have recently met.*

PAY "ATTENTION"

In our family, the notion of following up was decreed by Grandmother Fay, who never let a day go by without giving out "attentions," as she called them, to anyone who had reached out to her in any way. If someone was helpful or nice—by lending her an umbrella during a heavy downpour or offering her a compliment or carrying her all-too heavy groceries—that person would, without fail, receive a thank-you call or letter from Fay. And anyone who called Fay to thank her for something received a thank-you call in return, which could go on and on ad infinitum!

Fay kept ample notes and lists about everything in her life, and she spent a large portion of each day corresponding with people. In return, she was a most beloved person with a wealth of friends. Fay's motive behind her "attentions" was simply to make sure everyone in her life felt loved and appreciated. Although she loved doing it, Fay kept up with people and thanked them constantly because she felt that it was the right thing to do—she had an obligation to tell people she appreciated their efforts.

While the rigidity of feeling that one "should" send thank-you cards for even the most minuscule benevolent acts originated in the pages of early etiquette books, the motives for doing so were genuinely based. As we learned from our good friend and etiquette expert Letitia Baldridge, etiquette is really centered around kindness and thoughtfulness . . . and who can find fault with that? "The great and wonderful thing about rules of etiquette," she says, "is that they were put in place by the leaders of our civilization not as an exercise in intimidation, but to make to make people feel comfortable, relaxed, and secure in their behavior, and to show them how to make others feel comfortable, too."

Trust us, it didn't always feel that way in our family, especially after a cramp-inducing Christmas afternoon of writing thank-you notes, but later in life, armed with a new, more adult-driven understanding of the Letitia Baldridge perspective, Grandma Fay's legacy of writing expressive, creative, and kind letters became an art and a pleasure for all of us, once we were able to leave the obligatory "should" part of it behind.

While you are hoping to build friendships or maintaining long-standing ones, being a good correspondent will help you make and keep friends more than anything else. It is something that you can start to do at any time, without excessive time or money expenditure, and regardless of your communication skills. The key is to find a method that feels comfortable to you and your friend. Then all you have to do is pay "attention."

☐ *Replenish your supply of note cards*
and stamps, then mail a friend some "attention."

Express Your Affection

In business, follow-up literally follows some action—it is done to clarify goals after a meeting, provide information needed to close a deal, or give colleagues an agenda. There is a protocol to be followed. In friendship, follow-up is not quite so rigid, and can be practiced more creatively—and without a schedule. The benefits are less tangible; they cannot (and should not) be measured, but you will feel the rewards of having done so with as much (or more) pleasure as you would receive from a promotion or a raise!

One of the nicest (and easiest) forms of friendly follow-up is simply the expression of your warm feelings for someone. This may take the form of a compliment, it might be acting on the urge to say "hello" to an acquaintance you haven't seen in a while, or it might just feel right to give a longtime confidante a warm hug. You'll have to gauge what level of affection is right for the particular relationship.

Whatever means you choose to express your affection, your sincerity and warmth will be clear. The result will be to encourage a new relationship or deepen an existing one.

☐ *Hug a dear friend . . . like you mean it!*

THE
"BON" BAKERS

Just after I got out of the army in 1953, I moved to Houston, Texas. I was in a new town, working long hours at Foley's, a large department store. Through a friend of a friend, I was fortunate enough to be placed on a party list as an "eligible bachelor," which gave a much-needed boost to my nascent social life.

One of my dates was a lovely young woman named Bonner Baker. I was her escort quite a few times and got to know her parents as well. They were always very hospitable to me. As Foley's china buyer, I was interested in seeing what kinds of dishes and crystal people had in their homes, and Mrs. Baker showed me her collection.

Over time I got to know many of the Baker clan in Houston, including Lovett and JoAnne Baker and Bonner's brother, Jim Baker (who became secretary of state and secretary of the treasury under President George H.W. Bush.) The whole family welcomed me and helped make my days in Houston happy ones.

Recently, I realized that I wanted to tell the Bakers how much their family had meant to me all those years ago. Though I hadn't seen any of them for some years. I decided to write them a letter. I had no motive other than to express myself. It felt great to do so.

THINK SMALL BUT SINCERE

Showing your appreciation to a friend doesn't have to be a grand gesture. It's more important to do it swiftly and sincerely. If you want to thank a friend for listening to you ramble on and on while you dished out the sordid details of a recently failed romance, simply pick up the phone and say thank you. No elaborate dinner date, replete with a string quartet and majestic views of the sunset is needed. That kind of an evening might have saved your lackluster romance—especially if a horse-and-carriage ride was thrown in—but it will only overwhelm your friend. Besides picking up the phone, there are many other small gestures that can effectively communicate your appreciation:

- *Send a note.* It doesn't matter whether you're technologically savvy or prefer sending letters the old-fashioned way. Send an e-mail, fax a letter, mail a postcard or note; no matter what method you choose, it's a failsafe way of letting someone know you care.

- *Give a (small) gift.* How delightful it is to receive a gift out of the blue. Something small but meaningful—a photograph of the two of you, a book you think he'd enjoy, or a bouquet of blooms you know she loves—would do the trick. If you see something that is just right, send it—no need to wait for an occasion.

- *Help out.* If you know a friend is in need, why not help out? Offer to take care of his kids for an evening or bring her a home-cooked meal.

- *Offer congratulations.* Your friend will be touched that you noticed his accomplishments—both large and small.

In good times and in bad, find a way that works for you—but do find a way—to tell your friends how much they mean to you: give compliments, hugs, praise, and point out all the positive reasons why you are interested in, inspired by, and comforted by their friendship. Expression is the ultimate act of friendship—one that will give you immense pleasure and will come back to you in spades. Shout it from the rooftops! Being and having a friend is one of life's best rewards. Even the smallest gesture of appreciation will have great returns.

☐ *Send a postcard to a friend just to say "I'm thinking of you."*

FILE-FRIENDLY

I love to organize—and that urge extends to other people's things as much as my own! When my friend Jennifer Pate, a recent mother of two, was in dire need of cleaning up her desk, I knew I had something to offer. Instead of a lunch date, I offered to set up Jennifer's filing system. As I delved into her piles of paper, Jennifer nursed her newborn and we chatted. Jennifer had showed her friendship for me in the past in multiple ways, some more action-oriented than expressed, like referring me to a new friend or coming early to a dinner party to help me set up. Helping Jennifer adjust to her life as a new mommy was much more meaningful for both of us than had I simply sent a card or gift.

GIVE COMPLIMENTS

It takes such little effort to compliment someone. "You are a great e-mailer" or "You always make people feel so welcome" can be things that don't occur to the best correspondent or host. In these cases, when the compliment is about something the other person hasn't thought of as being terribly worthy or important, it's even better. If you begin to speak your mind to people sincerely, you will help abolish one of the most despicable misuses of social interaction: the empty compliment.

If you've ever been on the receiving end of a compliment or declaration of praise, love, or gratitude, you know that it feels good. One reason such expressions are so pleasing is because we all know that it isn't always so easy to say what's on your mind, directly, to the person whom you want to hear it. This is precisely why it means so much when you do take the time to recognize all the little things your friend does that makes you happy.

☐ *Compliment a friend today.*

DON'T DROP THE BALL

The first time you should follow-up in a friendship is immediately after you meet someone that you would like to get to know better. This is the moment when not "dropping the ball" is crucial; it's important not to wait until too long after the first encounter—so that it is fresh in both of your minds—to show your enthusiasm for moving your friendship forward. Similarly, if you told this new acquaintance that you would be happy to do something for him or her, now's the time to do it.

Whatever means of contact you are comfortable using is fine, as long as you communicate how much you enjoyed meeting the person and suggest that you see each other again in the near future to continue your dialogue. Refer to something that you talked about or any common bond that was created to build a bridge between your initial meet-and-greet and the second time you get together.

A note, too, about tardiness: if you are unable to make a speedy follow-up, the worst solution is to forget about it and allow the friendship to evaporate. Instead, follow-up late.

As in all other situations, be honest and sincere. When you make your follow-up, don't waste a great deal of time on apology and recrimination. Remind the other person of your prior contact and re-establish the connection. If it was a genuine connection, the person will appreciate your effort and you can pick up where you left off.

If you are concerned that your follow-up might seem a little aggressive or that someone might be bothered by hearing from you, know this: it's better to be late than never. Besides, everyone appreciates being appreciated!

☐ *If you enjoyed making a new acquaintance, follow through by saying so.*

The late and legendary businessman Stanley Marcus, my mentor, used to collect postcards and travel with them. While en route, he would jot down a few lines then send them at the next destination, just to say hello. Friends would be surprised and pleased when the cards arrived.

Now his granddaughter, Allison, who is Sally's oldest friend and a professional photographer, has developed her own version of the tradition. She sends twenty-five to thirty postcards per month created by hand from her photographs. With just a few sentences, Allison keeps in touch with people while summing up her whereabouts or experiences in an image.

RULE #43

BE SPECIFIC—AND BRIEF

When writing a note to someone, be it a "thank you" or a "nice to meet you," always refer to the gesture or incident you are writing about. Just as in conversation, where speaking in specifics beats pointless small talk, so in your written correspondence, details make the message more authentic. If someone has done a kind turn, and you want to let them know you appreciated it, you might say, "Thank you for introducing me to Mark," or "It was so nice of you to arrange that baby shower for Lynne." If you recently met someone you would like to see again, mention something about your interaction that you both clearly took pleasure in: "I really enjoyed our chat about Surrealist art."

Be warm, open, friendly—and brief. Once you have made your point, you're done—there is no need to write a four-page letter just to say, "It was nice to meet you." (Save the enthusiasm for the next time you meet in person.)

If you choose to send a birthday or holiday greeting to maintain your connection, add a short note: "Just wanted to wish you a lovely birthday." For longstanding but long-distance friends, you might make reference to the last time you got together. Don't feel pressured to fill the white space—the fact that you've

☐ *Send a handwritten thank-you card to a friend.*

There was a time in my life when I used to like to send long missives to my parents that detailed everything I'd been doing—almost like a journal. In return, they would write similarly long responses. It seemed that writing these free-form letters to each other created a unique state of mind in which we all felt free to express ourselves quite intimately—and I have come to suspect that we might have revealed more of ourselves to each other because of it.

Today I still have those letters we exchanged—and reading through them never fails to remind me of how lucky we are to have expressed our feelings in writing, so that I now have a tangible record of our relationship that I will always cherish.

LET 'EM OFF THE HOOK

Playing hooky from work to eat an entire pint of ice cream while watching reruns of *Dallas*. Buying a pair of five-hundred dollar Manolos on credit when, really, you only have fifty bucks to your name. "Borrowing" your sister's favorite cashmere sweater without telling her. These are all situations that inspire feelings of guilt. Maintaining a friendship with someone shouldn't. Period.

Friendships aren't based on a tit-for-tat exchange system, which is why, when you choose to send a long e-mail or letter, it's nice to let people off the hook and let them know that you don't expect them to respond in kind if they can't or don't want to. Write "Read/respond when you can" or "No response necessary" at the top of the letter or as the subject line of an e-mail to get this across. Ted Cross, a family friend, takes a more amusing approach, attaching a note to a clipping that says: "Don't you dare respond to this." A rule of thumb in writing a quick e-mail to simply touch base with a friend is to limit the length to what will fit on a sticky note (a small one).

Perhaps the only thing worse than feeling obligated to respond to someone's casually written letter is having to explain to your sister how her sweater "accidentally" ended up in your closet.

☐ *Send a friend a "don't you dare respond" e-mail.*

PICK UP THE PHONE

Letter writing reigned supreme over the telephone for decades because of cost. Before the ubiquity of cell phones and telecom conglomerates forced the price of phone calls down to a minimum, people saved long-distance or overseas calls for special occasions.

Nowadays, phone conversations, or at least leaving a message or voice mail, are a dependable and direct way to follow-up—just short of meeting in person. Phone calls allow you to hear the person's voice, which makes the connection more personal than an e-mail.

In telephone contact, understand that some people can't or don't like to chat on the phone. At the beginning of a phone call, always ask if it's convenient to talk before launching into a conversation. If you have a friendship with someone who does enjoy talking on the phone, try to set up "appointment times," as if you were meeting in person, that are convenient for both of you to talk.

☐ *If you find yourself passing through a city where a friend lives, give him or her a call and re-connect. Make it clear you don't expect to get together but just wanted to say hello.*

PRESS "SEND"

At its best, e-mail allows you to do all of the things that you can do in a letter and more, with ease and no postage cost. Instead of clipping an article, you can cut and paste it, or send a link directly to a Web site. Instead of buying an assortment of birthday cards, you can custom design them or send an e-mail greeting through a greeting card site. You can attach digital photos or audio files without having to take time to print doubles and put them in an envelope. You can print out important e-mails and save them, so they can be reread and archived like letters.

E-mail has changed the way people approach corresponding. Because of its ease, people are often more conscientious about following up and keeping in contact with friends. Arguably, e-mail has improved friendship capacity for everyone who uses it.

At its worst, though, e-mail's ease can make people somewhat lazy about the more important aspects of friendship or the communication means appropriate for a situation. One must be ever-prudent not to rely upon e-mail to replace real, live interaction with others, whether by phone or in person, but to use it in concert with these means.

☐ *Send an e-card to a close friend.*

SEND YOUR CONDOLENCES

As wonderful and easy as it makes keeping in touch, e-mail is simply not suitable for certain kinds of connecting. It is a more casual medium, and it is not particularly private. Therefore, any sensitive, emotional, or confidential topics should not be dealt with via e-mail. (Especially since e-mail is often sent from work, where it may be monitored, you should be careful not to send any personal messages this way.)

A significant gift requires a handwritten note sent by post. The effort you make acknowledges the effort the sender made, and shows your appreciation.

Condolences must always be sent via handwritten note. The formality of the message reflects its gravity and shows respect for the situation. (In a note of condolence, be sure to follow Rule #45 and refer specifically to a fine quality or memory you have of the departed.)

☐ *If a friend of yours is going through a difficult time*
(or has just lost a family member), send a thoughtful card, not an e-mail.

BE CREATIVE WITH YOUR FOLLOW-UP

You need not stick with the basic phone call, e-mail, note formula for follow-up—there are plenty of other creative ideas you can use to connect with someone! Just be sure that the method you choose is appropriate for the nature of the relationship. Here are some ideas:

- *Clippings:* Sending magazine or newspaper clippings that refer to a conversation you had with someone or that just made you think of that person is a follow-up method used successfully by grandmothers and CEOs alike. An e-mail with a link in it is the high-tech version of this form of follow-up!

- *Referrals:* These work for both purely personal contacts (put one friend newly arrived from Italy in contact with another Italian friend who has been here a long time) and for mixed personal-business relationships (refer a friend looking for a personal trainer to a trainer you have worked well with).

- *Events:* If you hear of an upcoming event that you know someone would like, send him the details. ("Did you know that author you mentioned is reading at the public library on Tuesday?")

☐ *If you read an interesting article, send it to an old friend you know will find it interesting—and a potential friend who might.*

A LIFETIME
OF HAPPY TALKING

Dorothy Rodgers, author and wife of the famous composer Richard Rodgers (Oklahoma, South Pacific, The King and I, *and* The Sound of Music)*, wrote a book called* My Favorite Things, *which was published while I was a buyer at Neiman Marcus in the 1960s.*

Stanley Marcus suggested that Neiman Marcus introduce the book in the Dallas store and feature it in one of our mailings, which was an unusual offering for the non-bookstore. Mrs. Rodgers came to Dallas for the event with her husband, who later said that it was the first time he had ever traveled with his wife to support her as the honored guest, rather than the other way around.

Following the very successful book launching, my wife and I were invited to dinner at the Marcuses with Dorothy and Richard Rodgers. As I was a very young buyer, it was a thrill to be invited to the boss's house and to be in such distinguished company.

In a very friendly dinner conversation, during which Mr. Rodgers asked me to call him "Dick," I reminded him that we had met in New Haven in 1949 when South Pacific *was playing its pre-Broadway try-out at the Shubert Theater. My date for the junior prom had a friend who* was an understudy in the show, so we had snuck into the theater to watch some of the rehearsals. While there we had met Mr. Rodgers, Mary Martin, Ezio Pinza, and the other stars of the play. Little did I dream that such a chance meeting would help me to make a new friend many years later.

At the end of the evening, Dick and Dorothy Rodgers were very appreciative of our work on behalf of her book and made us promise to let them know when we were going to be in New York so that we could see them again.

So often when people tell you to call them or "keep in touch," they don't really mean it, but somehow, I believed they were sincere. If they didn't mean it, I'll never know, because I did what they asked, and followed up: I wrote to tell them how much we had enjoyed meeting them and said that we would be in New York in four weeks. I didn't say that we would like to see them, because I didn't want to pressure them or push the "follow-up" too far. A week later we received a wonderful invitation from Dorothy to come for cocktails one night during our trip.

We went, had a wonderful time, met some interesting friends of theirs, and embarked upon a friendship, that lasted throughout our lives.

RULE #49

MAKE A DATE

No matter what follow-up method you choose, if your goal is to see the person again, be sure to suggest a get-together before too long. Vague communications will get you nothing more than a feeling of goodwill, and even that will dissipate if you make the mistake of repeatedly trying to connect through such impersonal messages as forwarded jokes.

Instead, make a plan. Don't write, "Hope to see you soon." A better idea is, "We would love to see you. Please join us for brunch on March 5." If the person lives far away, but you want to convey your interest in becoming friends, let her know: "If you're going to be in town again, please let me know so we can plan a lunch or dinner." Similarly, if you are the one traveling, try something like, "I am going to be in Toronto during the last week of July; if you're free, perhaps we could meet for a coffee." This lets the person know you're available to meet, but without any pressure.

These kinds of invitations are flattering and will usually be met with enthusiasm—in which case you are well on your way to a warm friendship.

☐ *Before you follow-up, think about the circumstances under which you'd like to see this person again and include a suggestion in your message.*

RULE #50

GIVE A LITTLE

There are lots of occasions when a small gift is a great way to say "thank you" or "I'm thinking of you." Some examples:

- When a friend or acquaintance has done you a favor
- To convey appreciation for an invitation
- If you know someone is feeling blue
- Because you know it will make a friend laugh

These gifts should never be lavish, and they should always be given without expectation of reciprocation. Some ideas:

- A paperback copy of a classic
- A music CD you created
- An amusing tchotchke
- A box of homemade cookies
- A packet of seeds
- A candle

Be spontaneous, and your generosity will come back to you in unexpected ways.

☐ *The next time you spot a little something*
you know a friend would like, get it for him.

CHAPTER SIX

Deepen the Connection

Getting to know you,
Getting to know all about you.
Getting to like you,
Getting to hope you like me.

—OSCAR HAMMERSTEIN, *THE KING AND I*

Life is too short to spend it paddling around in the shallow water. In order to experience the wonders of friendship, you have to take the plunge and head for deeper waters. While there are several different ways to deepen a friendship, a change in context is sometimes all that's needed to elevate your sense of commitment. Getting out of the kiddie pool and into the ocean, for example, may be just what you need to see if your friendship will sink or swim. (Of course, we're betting on the latter.)

```
┌─────────────────────────┐
│  ┌───────────────────┐  │
│  │ RULE  │ #51        │  │
│  └───────────────────┘  │
└─────────────────────────┘
```

KEEP OLD FRIENDS

There are some friends with whom, even though you may not have seen each other in years, you can pick up exactly where the two of you left off, with no awkward stuttering or uncomfortable pauses. Chances are, these kinds of friends are among your closest: the bond that you share is so strong that it cannot be eroded by time, distance, or life's distractions and inconveniences. Don't make the mistake of neglecting or ignoring these perfectly good friendships in your quest to meet new people. Instead, make the effort to keep in touch via mail or e-mail, and when you can, visit in person.

These are the relationships you cherish, the friends you can always count on, the confidants you turn to during a crisis. Let these friends know how much you value them by freely telling them so—as often as you can!

☐ *Call an old friend just to say "hi."*

RULE | #52

UPDATE YOUR EXPERIENCES

No matter what the circumstances or the seminal moment that originally brought you and a friend together—being stuck in an airport or sharing laughs over a few cocktails or simply being in the right place and the right time—and no matter how comfortable and easy the relationship is as a result of your common bond, it cannot be sustained forever without updated experiences.

Keeping up with friends by phone, mail, and e-mail is the first step in making sure that your knowledge of their lives does not remain mired in the past. Not that there's anything wrong with the past; in fact, reflecting upon it and sharing memories with an old friend is a wonderful way to maintain a friendship. Talking with that one other person who shared some experience or place in time with you keeps that moment alive in both of your minds. However, lingering too much on the past will prevent you from moving forward into a new era with your friend. Seize every opportunity to create new memories with an old friend.

When Charlie Sanders, a good friend of Roger's from Cambridge in the 1960s, came to the London opening of *Kiss Me, Kate* (in which he also invested), he and Roger were in for an unprecedented catch-up. For the preceeding thirty years, they had kept up by phone and mail, seeing each other approximately once per year when Charlie passed through Dallas. Roger invited Charlie on a weekend jaunt from London to Bilbao,

Spain, with Roger Berlind, the co-producer of the play, and his wife. On this adventure, they enjoyed and exchanged opinions about art, architecture, food, and wine, in the process learning much that they hadn't known about each other in all of the years of their friendship. Introducing Charlie to the Berlinds, friends from more recent years, also served to update the relationship. Their memories now extend well beyond their time in Cambridge.

Whether you plan a trip or a simple barbecue in your backyard, bring old friends into your current life. Make an effort to become involved in their latest endeavors. It might seem like enough to merely re-connect with an old friend once a year at a conference or reunion, but the friendship will be more rewarding if you add new experiences rather than simply reliving the old.

□ *Have a conversation with an old friend in which the two of you only talk about your present-day endeavors.*

RE-CONNECTING WITH A CHILDHOOD FRIEND

When I was eleven years old, I went to Wyonegonic Camp in Denmark, Maine, the oldest girls' summer camp in the USA, and I met a dear friend, Vezna Gottwald. Vezna and I performed in The Wizard of Oz together (she was Dorothy, I was the Scarecrow), and I visited her in New York after camp was over.

Like many friends from these early, somewhat fleeting moments in our childhood, Venza and I lost touch. But last year, we were treated to an amazing reunion, set up by my parents and our mutual friend, Mimi Kilgore, who had learned that Vezna and I lived in the same city.

Mimi sent me the catalogue of Vezna's paintings (she is now a professional painter), and we spoke on the phone. The very next weekend, we spent a full day catching up and learning about what we had missed in the previous twenty-three years. Though our lives had been different, we still had many things in common, and most of all, enjoyed each others' company. We're thrilled to be reconnected, and though it's an effort to strike up a new friendship as adults, our long-ago childhood relationship provides a sturdy foundation for conversation and connection. It's nice to be a grown-up with a childlike appreciation for an old kinship.

TRANSFORM A PASSIVE
CONTACT INTO A FRIEND

Let's assume that for the last two months you have regularly attended a photography seminar. While waiting for your class to start, you have exchanged greetings and had a few enjoyable, albeit quick, conversations with another person. Unfortunately, your small talk banter has remained just that, even though you suspect that the two of you may share common interests that extend beyond photography. It's time for you to transform this "passive contact" (anyone that you see on a regular basis but fail to connect with) into a friend.

So, for example, rather than banking on the fact that you'll see this person again at the next seminar, go out of your way to exchange contact information and make a plan to do something outside of your regular meeting place. If the new venue provides an opportunity to talk—lunch in a restaurant versus seeing a movie—you will certainly get to know the person better. Or, you may want to build on your already established commonality and attend a gallery opening or go out and shoot some photos together. This shared interest is a great foundation and, hey, you may perfect your focus while you're at it.

☐ *The next time you say hello to a passive contact, ask if he or she would like to get together outside of your regular meeting place.*

MAINTAIN LONG-DISTANCE RELATIONSHIPS

You probably have many friends in your life that you don't get to spend time with very often simply because you are separated by distance. Typically, you see these friends at major life events, like weddings, reunions, and birthday parties, though much of your friendship is based on the occasional phone call or end-of-year holiday card. Unless you are an exceptionally diligent letter writer, it may be difficult to fill each other in on the intimate day-to-day aspects of your life.

The best way to deepen the connection with these important but faraway friends is to go out of your way to create periodic visits with them, once a year or so. This may mean taking a special trip somewhere, if only for a day or a weekend, or coordinating a meeting at a halfway point. If you travel to a city that's close to where a good friend lives, tack on a few extra driving hours to see her. Yes, this requires a bit more planning than dropping a card in the mail and, yes, it may also necessitate spending more than a three cents a minute to hear your friend's voice but, trust us, the payoff will be priceless. Even one hour of shared time will elevate the quality of your friendship for months and years to come.

☐ *Plan a trip to visit one of your faraway friends.*

THE
ROOMMATE AND I

One year, Chrissy Coughlin, my roommate from high school, flew from the East Coast to Los Angeles for the Grammy Awards. To my delight, she invited me to join her. The evening's adventures ended up rivaling our exploits from school. Over the course of the evening, she and I exchanged impressions of the culture of celebrity, the music industry, and city life. This kind of concentrated discovery would not have happened in a periodic e-mail exchange or even while catching up at a wedding. We learned more about each other as adults, apart from the teenagers we once knew, and became closer for it.

BE INTIMATE

We're not suggesting you pop the champagne and groove to Barry White. We do advocate, though, that you and your friend start "dating," that is, make meeting times to regularly see each other. Why? These meetings, which can be based around a shared interest or common goal, produce stability and reliability within a relationship and further solidify your bond with one another. A "meeting" can be as formal as a weekly sit-down lunch or as casual as a Sunday stroll through the park. With a regularly anticipated meeting time, you sail past the superficial small talk (and recaps of past issues) and into the deeper waters of intimate dialogue. You and your friend have the opportunity to talk about and exchange thoughts on subjects beyond the broad brush strokes.

Another way of creating more intimacy in friendships (and by "intimacy" we simply mean "personal understanding") is to open your home to your friends. Once the doors to your personal abode have swung open, it's natural that your conversation will be more revealing. Just make sure you hide all the Barry White albums . . . unless you want to reveal more than just your friendly side.

☐ *If you don't already have a regular*
"date" with a good friend, make one.

MANAGE YOUR TIME COMMITMENTS

Sad but true, it's necessary to schedule—even in friendships. To get the most out of your day, not to mention your friendships, set aside blocks of time in your planner to see your friends. For example, every Saturday that they are both in Dallas, Roger has lunch with his friend Jacques Vroom. Although their friendship spans decades and originated in the workplace, it has been maintained through this regular catch-up.

We know, we know . . . you're wondering how can you possibly make all these dates when you barely have time for yourself and your family. How can you possibly make yet another commitment to yet another new friend, nevermind that she is wonderful and you have so much in common that you may as well have been twins separated at birth. "My schedule is already too full," you're saying as you throw your hands into the air. "Pretty soon, I'll have to start scheduling my dream time while I sleep!" When you think about it, though, with 1,440 minutes in a day, surely you can find a few for a good friend? Here are a few possibilities to budget your time into a regular face-to-face meeting:

- Meet for exercise or a walk one day a week.

- Car pool, bus, or take a subway together to a meeting you both regularly attend.

- Share a meal. (You have to eat, anyway.)

- Watch your favorite TV program or sporting event together.

- Catch up while you do your laundry.

- Meet for an afternoon cup of coffee.

- Make a joint appointment to get your hair cut (or your nails polished).

It's also important to realize that different levels of friendship require different levels of time commitment. Strangely enough, as our friend Sara Mosle put it in a *New York Times Magazine* essay, "The Importance of Being Busy," your closest friends could also be the people you see the least. With more formal friends, she wrote, you make plans weeks in advance, and you stick with the plans no matter what. "The unstated rule is that you can cancel only on those whom you genuinely like," she contends. "Only a true friend would understand."

Don't let this happen to you—make time for your friends.

☐ *For one week, jot down all the minutes (or hours) in which you are free. Now, creatively plan your social life around this "downtime."*

CHAT 'N' CHEW

For me, the daily lunch hour is one of the best times to see friends. Although I have regular lunches with a few close friends (like the aforementioned Jacques), if I have an opening in my schedule, I consult a list of people I keep hidden in my desk drawer that I'm constantly adding to—it's called the "Folks I Would Like to See More Of" list.

Stanley Marcus's "Good Guys Luncheon" was an annual event he created to gather his favorite male friends together. I attended for many years. It was great not only because it allowed Stanley to catch up with several of his friends at once, but because it created a shared experience for all of us that bonded some of the other folks to each other.

RULE #57

BE A HOST/HOSTESS

A terrific way for a busy person to catch up with friends is to host a group of them all together—also known as having a party. If you know how to make a mean margarita and a deliciously smooth guacamole dip, you already have the basic ingredients to throw a Mexican-themed fiesta. If beer and burgers is more your thing, why not have an impromptu backyard BBQ? Whatever your fancy, hosting a party can be an easy, fun, and creative way to surround yourself with the friends you love best. And, when you're inclusive with your invitations, it's also a great way to fold different people into the mix: your friends from work can mingle with your buddies from poker night, for example.

But, you may say, my apartment is too small or messy, or I hate to cook or I just don't have time to pull it all together. If that's the case, invite everyone to meet at a bar, restaurant, pool hall, or any place you can all descend upon with a minimum of planning, and where you can mingle unrestrictedly. Don't invite so many people that it becomes uncomfortably packed; do make time to talk to everyone you invited.

☐ *Create your own list of people you would like*
to see more of. Now, host a dinner party and invite them all.

SOCIALIZE CREATIVELY

If you're not one for parties, there are many other creative ways for you to be sociable. If, for example, you enjoy going to opera or the ballet, why not occasionally purchase an extra ticket or two and invite a friend to accompany you? If your close friends have already attended the season's production of *Swan Lake* with you a billion times, why not use the opportunity as a way to include someone else from your life?

Creating new and different experiences to share with friends can be as simple as trying a new restaurant together, as substantial as taking a trip or as adventurous as trying something completely new (trapeze classes or a day spent snorkeling). Whatever activity you decide to embark on, give it a creative twist: instead of simply meeting friends, organize a clothing swap where everyone brings a few unwanted articles and gets to make an exchange. Donate any leftovers to a resale shop or charity organization. Or, if you and a couple of your friends have an affinity for beer-battered catfish and roasted rainbow trout, skip the fish store and, for a change, go on a fishing trip to reel in your dinner. At the very least, you will return with great stories (and, hopefully, a full tummy, too).

Leave some room for spontaneity. If you and a friend are going to a bar that also happens to be located in the same neighborhood where another one of your friends lives, give her a call for a spur-of-the-moment invitation. Of course, this type of invitation, like any other, depends on the level of your friendship and whether or not the suggested activity is something your friend would enjoy. Whenever possible, tailor your interactions with friends according to what is best suited to their personalities. They will be the happier for it, and you will, too.

Like many of our suggested rules, going out of your way to create new experiences with your friends requires thought, action, and a willingness to change your typical routine. This change, however, will not only allow you the depth of friendships you are seeking, it will also make your life more interesting, too. Besides, everyone needs at least one heavily exaggerated fish tale.

☐ *Give an ordinary social gathering a creative, unexpected twist.*

FOODIE OUTINGS

Mitchell Peck and I principally knew each other through various Los Angeles friends, but when we started talking about ethnic food, we knew we had a special connection. Both of us had a real interest in getting to know foreign cultures through their traditional cuisines, and we found that we both spent a significant amount of time researching the best places in Los Angeles to sample them. So, we started a tradition of Ethnic Foodie Field Trips.

Every month, we gather a group of interested eaters to try the food of a culture other than our own. With the help of foodie message boards, like Chowhound.com and our local newspapers, we make an assessment about the best place to set up a banquet meal. Then we pick a date, send out an Evite, and take a field trip. It's a wonderful way to educate ourselves and our palates, and connect with our friends through an adventure we might not experience by ourselves.

RULE #59

BECOME A MATCHMAKER

The most obvious connections are based on areas of mutual interest. If you have a friend who is passionate about his collection of Hopi pottery, it's an obvious step to introduce him to your archeologist friend who is researching the Hopi tribe. But keep in mind that many a successful match is based on the theory that opposites attract. Perhaps your outdoorsy friend from work will make a connection with the poet who never leaves her house. Arrange for them to meet and be prepared for a surprise.

If you plan a one-on-one meeting for friends, it might be wise to keep the exposure limited. A quick coffee date or a lunch could be the appropriate venue. That way, if, Heaven forbid, they meet and discover an instant antipathy, they won't have to spend too much time in each other's company.

A group setting, like a dinner party, is another excellent way to introduce people to each other. Don't assume that your job is done when you send out the invitations. When you make introductions at the party, be sure to give these potential friends a basis for communication beyond small talk. In these situations, you are the connector and, therefore, have the obligation to initiate the conversation.

☐ *Set up a visit between two friends of yours who have similar interests.*

BOHEMIANS
AND HILLBILLIES

A few years ago, my friend Van Galbraith, a former U.S. ambassador to France, invited me to go with him and his friend William F. Buckley, Jr. to the Bohemian Grove, an exclusive retreat in a large Sequoia forest near San Francisco. The Bohemian Club operates "camps" for its members and their guests each summer, and I was lucky enough to join Van and Bill in the "Hillbilly Camp."

Van and I had not seen each other in a while because I was in the midst of producing Crazy For You *on Broadway, so he thought it would fun and interesting for us to get together at this place that was special to him. He also thought that the weekend would give me a chance to get to know Bill Buckley better, as we had gone to the same college but never spent any time together.*

It turned out that our four days of togetherness made for wonderful bonding with my old friend Van and discovery of a new friend in Bill. Bill was entertaining, thoughtful, intelligent, well informed, and contrary to my presuppositions, very interested in other people's opinions.

The Bohemian Grove adventure was full of many interesting and lively discussions, and this shared experience that Van created for us enhanced my friendship with him and allowed me to form a new, unexpected one with Bill, both of which continue to this day.

CHAPTER SEVEN

Give It Away

In the sweetness of friendship let there be laughter,
and sharing of pleasures.

—KAHLIL GIBRAN

Friendship is about giving for the sheer pleasure of making your friends happy—it is not about giving in order to receive. True friends do not portion out their affections according to what they are getting back, and they never keep score. The true beauty of friendship is that it is bottomless. You can give and give and give of yourself and the well of a successful friendship will never run dry. In fact, the more you give, the more you will receive in return.

DO A FAVOR

Quid pro quo. Tit for tat. I scratch your back, you scratch mine. What have you done for me lately? These are the kind of phrases that should never be uttered amongst friends. Unlike business relationships, friendships require you to give unselfishly, without expectation of getting anything in return. In an ideal world, when you do something nice for a friend, whether it is inviting him to a cabin for a weekend getaway, giving a small trinket as a token of your friendship, or offering a shoulder to cry on, it should make you feel good. That is your reward. If you like someone and can do that person a favor, don't hesitate: just do it. As the song goes, "that's what friends are for," right?

Sometimes this is easier said than done. Those of us who care deeply about our friendships expend a considerable effort in doing so, and it's often difficult not to want others to "do unto you" in the same manner. What we must all realize is that some people "do unto us" in very different ways than we "do unto them." And all the diverse expressions of friendship are valid. It's pointless to ponder whether or not you can repay a dinner party invitation with two cocktail parties or a letter with a phone call. Don't keep score, and you will be a happier person and a better friend.

There are many reasons why someone else's approach to friendship may be different from your own. Keep in mind that there are as many different types of personalities as there are friends, and each one may approach the relationship differently:

- A shy person is not as likely to feel as comfortable taking the initiative to make plans or keep in touch as you might be.

- A genuine introvert may find frequent contact with others to be exhausting or debilitating.

- Some people suffer from physical or emotional disabilities that limit their opportunities for intimacy.

- Some individuals have been lucky enough to usually be on the receiving end of friendly advances; they are unused to having to make the effort.

Whatever issues your potential friend faces, you can still express friendship, thoughtfulness, and gratitude. You can find ways to connect with each person and create a happy medium so that your needs are met, too. Remember, there are many people out there who, for one reason or another, don't, can't, or won't entertain or invite you out, and—guess what?—they are still your friends.

☐ *Do a favor for a friend.*

THE

GOOD DOCTOR

I had a friend who was a doctor, who was very interesting and entertaining but a little peculiar. Although he liked to go to parties and dinners at his many friends' homes, he simply didn't like to entertain in his own. Nevertheless, he was a very sought after dinner guest.

Over time, we all realized that he would never reciprocate our invitations, but we liked his company so much that we accepted it. We didn't keep score.

A few years ago, the doctor inherited a large piece of land in Chicago, which he sold immediately for many millions. It was about the same time that he retired from his medical practice. Suddenly, he had a lot more money and time than he had before.

One day he chartered the British Airways Concorde, invited forty-nine couples who had been his friends and hosts over the years, and took us all to London for a week, all expenses paid. Had we been keeping score, we would have found that all of our years of hosting were generously paid back in this one event. The doctor reciprocated his friendship in his own way—and in his own time!

RULE #61

DON'T KEEP SCORE

Each of us, for better or worse, has the potential to be a "score-keeper." The key is recognizing when or why you are prone to keeping score, and then avoiding doing so. If you fall in the category of someone who likes to entertain and be outgoing and is proactive about planmaking, you are at constant risk of not following the "Don't Keep Score" rule. Every once in a while, you may wonder when someone will reciprocate your invitation or why someone doesn't have you over more often. You might also "keep score on yourself" from time to time, agonizing about the way to properly reciprocate someone else's expression of friendship.

You may have a tendency to put more value on each interaction than other people do. But that is not a good enough reason to then evaluate, pass judgment on, or fuss about others' actions in this way. Doing so is a common, but unacceptable trap that only leads to disappointment.

Some people keep score because they are guilt-ridden and assume that others are judging their contribution. Others feel they are "owed" in all aspects of their lives, and thus keep a constant tally of those who are indebted to them. Those are the people who might go out of their way to introduce you to someone new, but then expect you to be forever grateful for the introduction. They are the kind of people who need credit, who can't enjoy the simple joy of generosity alone.

So, how can you avoid being a person who keeps score? First of all, you must not let the idea of payback come into play at all, whether you are on the giving or receiving end of an expression of friendship. Get out of the "who owes me" way of thinking.

Next, you must recognize and appreciate the ways that people reach out to you; this will help you do the same. You should assume that others are not keeping score either. If you do something in order to get credit or receive something in return, you are doing it for the wrong reason. Stop measuring your relationships; relax, be kind, and the world will suddenly seem more generous.

☐ *Perform a random act of kindness for a friend, acquaintance, or stranger.*

RULE #62

GO OUT ON A LIMB

Strong, silent types: listen up! You, too, shy wallflowers! If you have ever found yourself holding back your true feelings, not speaking out when something delights or upsets you, or assuming someone knows how you feel about them, please read on. (The rest of you can always use a refresher course, so you read on, too!) Whatever the reason for your reticence—be it a stern upbringing or a past rejection—here is the chance to change your inhibited ways. If this prospect makes you nervous, remind yourself that one of the best gifts of friendship is that you are allowed to express your true feelings come what may.

In friendship, the "rules" of expression are not nearly as clear as they are in business. Managers have guidelines for praising workers, know that it breeds an encouraging work environment, but are careful not to go overboard. Censuring a worker is even more regulated, almost always an official task done by the books, called a "warning."

Even in a romance, there are time-honored ways of telling someone how you feel about them to move the relationship forward or end it. Saying, "I love you" for the first time to a lover is a very big step, universally understood to mean that you want to be with that person.

"I love you" in friendship carries equal weight, but is rarely delivered with a heart-shaped box of chocolates or a bouquet of red roses. Friends must come up with other ways to send this message. They are likely to be more casual, and sometimes wordless. Yet many people resist expressing their love for friends because there isn't a set of ground rules for how it's done. This is actually the beauty of a friendly expression: there are no rules or hindrances. In fact, there doesn't have to be any particular reason for it and, better yet, it's almost always appreciated and almost never scorned (another win for friendship over romance). There are no token phrases or rote responses in friendship that you deliver because you "have to." No friend is waiting for you to tell him that you really like spending time with him or particularly enjoy hearing his take on a subject, so when you offer up your feelings in such a way, it's very meaningful.

If you are somewhat shy or not used to speaking your mind in such a way, you should be comforted to know that your friends will appreciate your expressions even more, precisely because they are unexpected. Go out on a limb whenever you can to let people know how profoundly you appreciate them, and we guarantee you that it will come back to you in spades.

☐ *Tell a friend how much his or her friendship means to you.*

ADDRESS AN IMBALANCE

You may be familiar with the saying, "It takes two to tango." Sometimes the dance of friendship, however, can become a tangled mess, with both partners going in different directions at the same time or, worse, with one friend leading all the time and the other blithely unaware of the imbalance. We know you are not keeping score, but if you feel that you are giving much more than your friend or, worse, he is actively doing something that makes you unhappy or uncomfortable, you should not only seriously evaluate the relationship but you must address the situation, too.

Confronting an uncomfortable situation does not necessarily mean that the two of you are going to come to blows or that the friendship will go down in a fiery argument of mean-spirited comments, tears, and soap-opera-inspired dramatics—at least, we hope not. If you can tactfully tell your friend how you feel about whatever issue is at hand you should be able to have a reasonable discussion. If, for example, you find yourself doing and saying too much in a friendship, making every invitation, and always taking the initiative while your friend makes little to no attempt to reciprocate, or even avoids you, you might say, "You know, the last few times we have gotten together, I've called you to make the plan. I know how busy you are, so why don't you call me next when it's most convenient for you." This is a non-confrontational way to put the ball in your friend's court while expressing your needs. If you're prepared to be more direct, you might tell your friend that you're sensing a bit of reluctance on her part to participate in the friendship: is anything wrong that she'd like to talk about? Whatever phraseology you use, communicating that the situation is bothering you is absolutely essential; otherwise, you will become resentful and the relationship will turn very toxic very fast.

Of course, with one friendship, you may decide that the one-sidedness is acceptable, while another may prove too unsatisfying to continue. So long as your "dancing" partner doesn't abandon you on the dance floor all together, you can always find new ways to work with one another.

☐ *Come clean to a friend and tell him or her*
something that you've been wanting to say for quite some time.

CHAPTER EIGHT

The Ebb and Flow of Friendships

An eye for an eye makes the whole world blind.
—MAHATMA GANDHI

As with everything in life, friendships change and evolve over time. Over the course of a lifetime, a particular friendship may start out casual, become much closer, be taken for granted for a while, then be renewed. There are many possible paths for a friendship to take, depending on the natures and circumstances of the people involved.

Similarly, the quantity and quality of friendships you will experience in life may change. Sometimes you may be flush with friends, while other times you may not. During the fallow times, it helps to know that these waxings and wanings are just part of life—as long as you are genuine in your dealings, you will have the friends you need.

ACCEPT THE EBB AND FLOW

Rivers are fascinating. They are ever-changing, shifting, and evolving; as weak and slow-moving as sap during the dry season but swollen and overflowing during the wet. The ebb and flow of friendships is as fluid as river water—and this is a very good thing. If life was static and our friendships never changed, there would be no growth.

Some friends, like the neighbor who lived across from your home when you were five years old or the guy with whom you shared a cubicle at your very first job, exit your life almost as quickly as they entered it. Others who were once extremely close and meaningful to you may slowly fade away, due to any number of circumstances, situational or emotional. And happily, some friends, after being absent for an extended period of time, may re-enter your life when you least expect it. Occasionally, a single friendship may pass through any one of these stages, maybe even a few times.

It is exactly this kind of fluidity that makes friendship so unique and beautiful. Once you accept and value the flow of friendship, you will have the freedom to let it naturally run its course. Just like a river, a true friendship doesn't have to know where it is going to get there; it simply creates its own path along the way.

☐ *Let go of any resentment you may feel about a waning friendship.*

BE A FRIEND FIRST AND A
BUSINESS PARTNER SECOND

Some friendships naturally transform into a working business partnership. If you value your friendship, you must remember that you are a friend first and a business partner second. That said, do not enter lightly into a business dealing with a friend.

Some people mask an interest in doing business with you with a friendly approach. These folks have the equation backward: they want you as a business partner first and a friend second. Nothing positive will come out of gambling on a business proposition that uses friendship as ante. If, however, you are friends first, you and your friend can engage in an honest dialogue about the possible risks and potential pitfalls (financial and otherwise) of doing business together.

If you are considering doing business with a friend, you must always ask yourself, "What's the worst thing that can happen?" If the risk is too great, find someone else to do business with and keep your friendship alive.

☐ *Create a "friendship" clause for any business contract you sign with a friend that details how you will protect your friendship if the business deal goes awry.*

When I worked as Steven Spielberg's assistant, some people inevitably thought I might help them get access to the famous filmmaker. At first, it was difficult and uncomfortable to try to distinguish between people who genuinely wanted to be my friend, and those who just wanted to know me because I knew someone famous.

While I couldn't blame people for being curious about my job (and my boss), I had to learn not to be naïve about these less-than-sincere friends. Unfortunately, I had to be guarded in the face of potential new friendships, and even so, I was often disappointed by people I thought were interested in me but turned out to be more interested in how knowing me might help them. In the process, I learned a valuable lesson about choosing friendships, recognizing the users, and still allowing yourself to open up to others.

Many people approach relationships with ulterior motives that sometimes they don't even recognize in themselves. Be honest with yourself and others about what you want out of a friendship. If it seems more like a business arrangement than a pure exchange of fun and commonalities, it probably should be kept in the office.

BE WARY OF A WOLF IN SHEEP'S CLOTHING

The popular Aesop's tale of a wolf dressed in sheep's clothing is one with an important lesson: appearances and well-intentioned gestures can be deceptive. Even the most thoughtful gift can conceal ulterior motives. So long as you are honest and upfront with each and every one of your relationships, however, you will be able to keep all the "wolves"—those people who use and abuse friendships for the sake of their own personal (and often times business-related) gain—at bay.

Of course, it is natural for friends to sometimes help one another with business-oriented endeavors and ventures. If, for example, one of your friends is a talented sculptor and another friend of yours owns an art gallery, it makes sense for you to introduce them to one another. It is another matter entirely to seek out a friendship with someone for the sole reason of advancing your own business-oriented agendas. Not only will the friendship be disingenuous and based on a false sense of trust but you'll be no better than the wolves you were trying to keep away.

Be direct and honest in all of your transactions and be wary of those individuals who appear untrustworthy. Chances are, if you look closely, you'll notice snarling teeth hidden beneath their otherwise smooth and friendly façade.

☐ *Shepherd your "flock" of friends carefully.*

SOUR
GRAPEFRUIT

I hadn't heard from B., an old high school friend, for a long time, and was delighted to receive a long letter bringing me up to date on his life since we'd last been in contact. He told me how much he valued our friendship and was sorry that he hadn't been in touch for so long. I was very flattered, but more than a little puzzled when I received a wonderful basket of grapefruit a few weeks later with a card saying, "To my old, old friend Roger—with great memories of our lives together at the Hill" (the school we'd both attended some fifty years ago). In his letter, B. mentioned that he was retired, and hoped to find some interesting work in the future.

I wrote to thank him for the grapefruit, and about a week later received a phone call from good old B. who "just wanted to say hello." I didn't have to wait very long for B. to finally get to the point, which was: "I've been thinking about it and believe that I would be well qualified to be head of the National Endowment for the Arts. Since your friend Clay Johnson is now at the White House, I'd like you to (not "would you consider" or "would you mind") have him talk about me to President Bush."

The grapefruit should have been the first clue that my "friend" was a wolf in sheep's clothing.

When I got into the business of producing Broadway musicals, I had to face the issue of whether and how to approach my friends as investors. Ultimately, I decided that the right way to proceed was to be scrupulously honest with them.

When I spoke to them about the opportunity to invest, I always explained the potential risk that they might not regain a penny of their investment. To me, the worst thing that could happen was losing my old friends. I told them, "I'd rather not have your money than lose your friendship." Most of them invested anyway, and fortunately all of them are still my friends.

LEARN TO LET GO

With the flow comes the ebb. We have all experienced a friendship that gradually dissolves—one that may have been a part of your life for a long time, but for whatever reason doesn't fit into it anymore. Less often, these friendships end because of an event, like an insurmountable disagreement. In each case, you make an evaluation of the friendship—either consciously or subconsciously—and take steps to make it more comfortably distant in your life.

Accepting the demise of friendship means being realistic about life's ups and downs. But what of loyalty, you might ask? What of sticking with your friends through thick and thin? Hear this: loyalty is an important, essential trait to being a good friend. However, we feel that taking a solemn oath that a-friend-now-is-a-friend-forever is more restrictive than helpful. People and situations inevitably change in ways that also alter friendships as well. You are entitled to amend your opinion about someone over time, whether or not the person has said or done something to directly affect you, or has simply turned into a person with values different from your own. If your friend jumps off a cliff, do you follow him or her? A pure loyalist might answer "yes." A healthier answer is "no." Even the best of friends may grow to find their value systems, once the same, are now completely different. Sometimes that disparity is stronger than any bond formed earlier in life, and phasing out a friendship on those grounds—something Sally refers to as "spring cleaning"—is okay.

The ebb and flow of friendship is never better examined than when a person from the past comes back into your life. Many times, we seek out these old friends if we're passing through their city or have a circumstantial reason to re-connect, while simple curiosity can often fuel the search as well. It is so interesting to find out how someone has changed, or more often than not, stayed the same. It's miraculous that we sometimes find ourselves in wonderful, adult friendships with people that may have missed several eras of our lives.

The opposite situation can be very unrewarding, if not existentially disappointing, if you aren't careful to shelter your feelings. Re-connecting with a long lost pal, only to find out that he is nowhere near as witty and energetic as he was in college, is no fun at all. No matter the turnout, reconnecting with old friends serves many purposes in our own personal self-growth, and can be valued as one of life's great experiences.

While learning to value the ebb and flow is a more esoteric concept than a hard-and-fast rule, it holds the key to enjoying all of the pleasures of friendship. Without the acceptance that friendships, like life, take twists and turns that aren't always pleasant, you risk falling into an endless cycle of getting hurt or feeling embittered. Friendships come and go, and that's entirely okay.

☐ *Come to terms with a friendship that has been dissolving for some time.*

For many years John Mullen and I were very good friends. Carolyn and I saw a lot of John and his wife, Ann, and we were lucky enough to have John design our pool house in Dallas and our summerhouse in Nantucket, for which he won an architectural award. He was a co-founder of The Container Store—in his spare time!

However, as each of us became busier with our work and growing families, we more or less drifted apart. There was no incident or problem, just the business of life. One year, we attended a Christmas party at the Mullens', having not seen them in a while, and it was that contact which made us both realize that we'd missed our time together. We quickly remedied that by taking our datebooks out at the party and making a future date for lunch. Since then, we've been able to simply pick up where we left off, and a valuable friendship has been revitalized.

WALK AWAY

While developing a friend is like nurturing a beautiful flower, it is a sad fact that some friendships simply won't take root no matter how much attention you lavish onto them. Sometimes the circumstances, timing, or chemistry is simply not conducive to a making a meaningful connection. Rather than watching a relationship like this slowly wither away, it's best to quickly nip it in the bud.

Do not make empty promises to call or get together. Even an unfortunate relationship deserves your sincerity and honesty.

But how can you tell if a potential friendship isn't meant to be? Usually, you just feel it, but there may be some signs. If, for example, you consistently cancel plans with someone just as often as you make them, you can safely assume that neither of you has any real interest in seeing one another. If you find that the two of you are having the same conversation each time you meet, perhaps you don't have much to say to one another.

If you realize that a relationship with someone is more like a struggling weed than a blossoming flower, walk away. You'll both be the happier for it.

☐ *Walk away from a friendship you'd rather not pursue further.*

THE ONCE-AND-MAYBE FUTURE FRIEND

Every once in a while, you may need to lower the volume on a friendship, temporarily or long term. Here are some techniques to send the message that you are no longer truly available:

• *Be elusive. Without being dishonest or hurtful, be hard to get in touch with or to make a date with—a comment like, "My life has gotten so busy, I just don't know when I'll be able to get together again" will probably do the trick.*

• *Be a little distant. Without being impolite, keep your interactions superficial; it will not be long before the other person steps back as well.*

• *Be direct. If the situation warrants, be brave and tell the person the truth: "Sometimes people and friendships change, and I'm sorry to have to say it, but I feel that I need some time apart."*

If you treat your once-and-maybe-future friend with respect and courtesy, the relationship can be dialed back without undue hurt or unpleasantness. And since you once had enough in common to be friends, the time may come when you'll find each other appealing again. If you've been careful of each other's feelings, renewing your relationship will be easy.

GO WITH THE FLOW

Have you ever closely watched a swan paddle across a still lake? It seems to glide atop the water, creating sleek ripples against the water's surface. If you were to look under the water, however, you'd see that its webbed feet are paddling frantically. A lot of work goes into propelling this fine-feathered friend forward—much more than you would think is possible.

A successful friendship is similar: it may look effortless and easy but both parties know how much work is required to keep it afloat. If you are able to go with the flow of a friendship—yielding to it when it needs to be nurtured and patiently overcoming emotional or situational hurdles when they arise, for example—you'll find that the requisite work is absolutely enjoyable. Working on something that really matters to you is never laborious or tedious, after all, and friendships are among life's greatest works!

Let's take a moment then, with all this talk of ebbing (and webbing!), to celebrate and honor all the friendships that make life worth living.

☐ *Take stock of all the friends in your life.*

LET THE SUN SHINE IN

The sun never shines behind closed doors. By this, we mean that if you don't make it a practice to keep your doors open to life, you will miss many wonderful opportunities to meet and make new friends and embrace the world around you. Letting the sun shine in requires opening your doors to the people around you and welcoming opportunities to connect with them in a meaningful way.

Keep your doors open and you will never experience a shortage of friendships—or joy—in your life.

☐ *Step outside and explore the new friendships and adventures that await you.*

The Lessons and Rewards of Connecting

As you've been reading this book and carefully checking off the to-do items, we're hoping you've already met several new acquaintances, some of whom are on their way to becoming good friends.

There are few experiences in life that rival the satisfactions and pleasures of friendship. Although friendship requires an effort, the rewards are immeasurable. This book is only a starting point. As you set out to make friends and enhance your already established relationships, you will find your own techniques. We wish you a lifetime of satisfying connections.